HOW · TO
· LOOK · AT ·
WILDLIFE

HOW · TO

·LOOK·AT· WILDLIFE

BOB GIBBONS

HAMLYN

Photographic Acknowledgements

Heather Angel;
Country Life Books/The Hamlyn Publishing Group Ltd.;
R Dickson/Natural Image;
John Feltwell/Wildlife Matters;
Robin Fletcher/Natural Image;
Bob Gibbons;
Liz and Bob Gibbons/Natural Image;
Frank Lane Picture Agency/Len Rue Jr.;
Peter Loughran/The Hamlyn Publishing Group Ltd.;
John Mason;
R. & M. Moiton;
Pat Morris/Wildlife Matters;
Nature Photographers Ltd:
Robin Bush
Frank V. Blackburn
Brinsley Burbridge
N. A. Callow
Colin Carver
Hugh Clark
Andrew Cleave
Ron Croucher
Michael Leach
C. K. Mylne
Owen Newman
W. S. Paton
Paul Sterry
Maurice Walker;
Paul Sterry;
Swift Picture Library, Ringwood/Mike Read;
Wildlife Studios Ltd.;
Peter Wilson;
Michael J. Woods.

Jacket photographs

Front: Peter Loughran/The Hamlyn Publishing Group Ltd.
Nature Photographers Ltd./Paul Sterry
Peter Wilson/Natural Image
Nature Photographers Ltd./Hugh Miles
Back: Peter Loughran/The Hamlyn Publishing Group Ltd.

Acknowledgements

The publishers would like to thank Stan Morse, Midsummer Books Limited, for the use of material from *The Country Life Book of the Natural History of the British Isles* Copyright © Midsummer Books Limited 1979; and John Feltwell for the use of material from *Discovering Doorstep Wildlife* Copyright © Templar Publishing 1985. All other material is the copyright of The Hamlyn Publishing Group Limited

Identification pages

The sizes of the animals and plants on these pages are not drawn to scale.
Key **bl:** body length **ws:** wing span **ht:** height **l:** length

Published in 1989 by
The Hamlyn Publishing Group Limited,
Michelin House, 81 Fulham Road, London SW3 6RB

ISBN 0 600 55692 1

Printed and bound by Graficromo s.a., Cordoba, Spain

CONTENTS

INTRODUCTION

Nowadays, there are more things to do than ever before – watching television, using computers, riding bicycles and playing sports are just a few of the possibilities. Yet an increasing number of people are taking up one of the most rewarding and simple of leisure activities – looking at wildlife. It is not hard to think why.

First, it is quite easy to get to places – some far-flung – and have a good look at a variety of wildlife. But it goes deeper than that, and reflects our need to keep in touch with the natural world, whether we live on a rural farm, or at the top of a high-rise block of flats. In fact, many of the keenest naturalists are urban-dwellers, getting out into the countryside at every possible opportunity, and coming back refreshed, ready to face city life again.

WHAT IS WILDLIFE?

When using the word 'wildlife' in this book, we do not mean only large animals, such as foxes or deer; we also mean birds, amphibians, insects, and even plants. The natural world is so closely inter-related that it really makes no sense at all to look at one part of nature in isolation from others. The more you understand how the countryside works, the better you are able to enjoy it, and the more hope we all have of conserving the best of it. You may, for example, enjoy looking at birds in particular, and get very engrossed in seeing as many bird species as possible. But no bird can survive without a suitable habitat to nest in, somewhere to roost and somewhere to go and feed in winter, and many birds need a whole range of habitats to help them survive. They will need to eat insects or plants, and may themselves be eaten by mammals or other birds.

The same applies to all other forms of life. That is why in this book wildlife is looked at in terms of habitats. The distinctive features of each habitat are detailed, and we see how the plants and animals live and interact together.

Right: *A beautiful kingfisher pauses before entering its nest hole with food for the young.*

Top: *A large hoverfly visits mint flowers for nectar.*

Above: *A common badger. This gregarious mammal has mainly nocturnal habits.*

The danger of looking at wildlife in this way is that one tends to think that wildlife only occurs in a single habitat, and has no contact with anything else. This is far from being the truth. Although many plants tend to grow in particular habitats, such as a woodland, they can often occur elsewhere, especially if the climate is only a little different. Many plants seem particularly to grow where two habitats meet – such as on the edge of a wood – rather than in any one habitat. More mobile animals, and birds, particularly migrating species, will quite visibly move from one habitat to another.

A newly-emerged dragonfly prepares to fly. Its emergence case is visible below it on the stem.

If you look at insects, many of which are not considered to be very mobile, you will often find that they depend on several habitats for their survival. Large dragonflies (*see* above) for example, lay their eggs into water, and the larval stages remain in water; but when the adult hatches out, it leaves the water, and seeks out sheltered drier places, such as woodland clearings or heathland for a time while its body hardens as it matures. Later the dragonflies will return to the water, but they will go off again searching for insects in all sorts of other habitats, and there are even one or two species that hibernate in woodland areas. Other insects also need a variety of habitats. The beautiful and intriguing longhorn beetles frequently spend their larval stages – often several years – in damp shaded dead wood, so they usually need old woodlands for this stage. However, when they hatch out, the adults seek out warm sunny areas with plenty of flowers, which usually only occur away from the wood, such as in a nearby meadow or marsh.

CONSERVING WILDLIFE

Clearly there is a need to protect *all* habitats, if wildlife is to survive and thrive. There is little point in putting a great deal of effort into conserving individual rare species, if all around the natural habitats are disappearing under barley or concrete. Much effort nowadays goes into trying to keep a representative sample of our best habitats, whether they are ancient woodland, heathland or mountainside, and therefore conserving all the species that go with them. Some examples will contain the rare species that sometimes occur in those habitats, while others will contain a wide range of the more common species, so that overall a reasonable balance is struck.

Unfortunately in much of the lowlands of western Europe, agriculture and development is so intense that only fragments of natural habitat remain. As we have already seen, most creatures need more than one habitat to survive, so this separation of habitats compounds the problem. At the same time, the fact that many plants and animals can only occur in widely separated sites, with hostile farmland in between, means that their populations become isolated. And extinction becomes a real possibility. More natural habitats are therefore vital, with hedges, lanes and shelter belts maintaining (or re-establishing) the connections between these isolated habitats.

STUDYING WILDLIFE

Never imagine that everything is known about our wildlife. There is a tremendous amount still to be discovered about wildlife in the countryside. The life-cycles and ecological requirements of most insects are still largely unknown, even those of some of the obvious groups, such as butterflies. If you develop an interest in one type of plant, insect, mollusc, or other creature in your area, you will soon discover questions that no-one can answer, and you may begin to answer some of them yourself.

Whether you look at wildlife just for the pleasure of seeing things, take up nature photography, or start to study in more detail, you can be sure that you will have an endless source of pleasure, that will probably last for the rest of your life.

Left: *Enthusiasts empty out the contents of a special live mammal trap to study what has been caught. This has to be done with extreme care to ensure no harm comes to any catch.*

Below: *It is hard to spot this beautifully camouflaged woodcock as it sits in its nest in woodland.*

DECIDUOUS WOODLAND

Deciduous woodlands are probably the most varied and species-rich of all the habitats that we have in north-west Europe.

For the amateur naturalist, a good deciduous wood is a place to see lots of different nesting birds, a wealth of wild flowers often in great abundance, hundreds of different species of insects including many butterflies, and as high a density of mammals as you can find anywhere. In autumn, woods are marvellous places for fungi which appear in all sorts of odd places, and if you start looking more closely still, you begin to find that they are also excellent places for lichens, mosses, liverworts, spiders, centipedes, and all manner of lesser known plants and animals.

A young doe fallow deer surprised early one morning in a forest ride.

The oak, a dominant tree in mixed woodland, in high summer.

TREES AND FLOWERS

The first thing that you notice about a wood is the trees – not just the fact that they are there, but which type of tree, how large and how densely packed together they are. Most people can recognize oak, ash, beech and a few others quite quickly, and realize, even if only subconsciously, that different woods have a different character, according to their trees. Most books talk about 'oakwoods', or 'beechwoods', and some woods are dominated by just one tree. In most natural woods, however, the character tends to be much more mixed, with several different trees jostling together, each doing best in conditions that suit it best. The deciduous woods that consist of one type of tree tend to have been planted or heavily managed over the centuries to favour just one species, and they are not really natural, even though the plants may be self-seeded. Nevertheless, the trees will support plenty of wildlife. Nuthatches and tree creepers forage on the tree trunks, searching for camouflaged moths and other insects. Up in the tree canopy, butterflies, like the speckled wood, flit from one patch of sunlight to another. Below, on the woodland floor, squirrels search for fallen nuts and seeds.

These main trees make up the canopy or 'roof' of the wood, and they have the greatest influence over what happens in the wood, since there are many insects, fungi, lichens, flowers and other organisms that particularly associate with one tree. There is usually a selection of smaller trees and shrubs too. Sometimes you can see layers of plants below the canopy, but most often you will only see a jumble of small trees, young larger trees, and shrubs, pushing together towards the light.

Above: *The fallen fruits of hornbeam on the forest floor where they are quickly found by mammals and birds.*

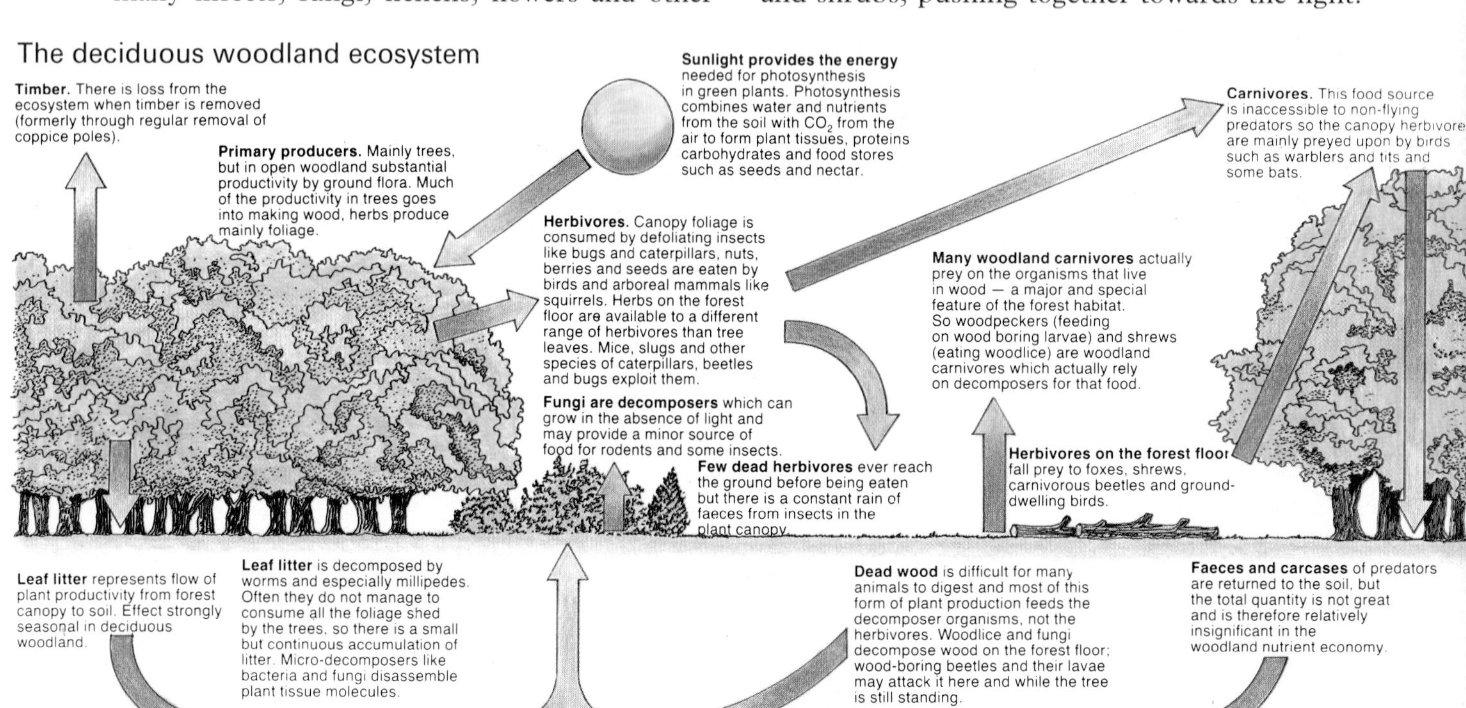

Left: *This diagram shows clearly how all the different aspects of nature inter-relate to each other.*

Above: *An old beech forest in autumn.*

An oakwood in spring, with all the bluebells in flower, is a breathtaking sight.

On the ground in woods, there will usually be masses of flowers, or at least the leaves of flowering plants. Most woodland flowers flower in the spring before the trees come into leaf, when the sun is blotted out and the light levels at the ground floor go down dramatically. A few plants flower very early in the year, in February or March. Most leave it as late as possible in the season, but always *before* the trees leaf out, so the peak period tends to be in late May. It is delightful for human observers, because it means that just about everything is out at once, in a sheet of mixed colours.

ENCOURAGING TREE GROWTH

You may occasionally notice that some trees and shrubs in a wood (or even *all* the trees and shrubs) may have a rather odd structure, with all the branches coming from ground level. Others, particularly those around the edge, may have strong single trunks up to about 2–3 metres, then branch out into a mass of smaller branches, with no separate main stem, the results of two ancient management practices: *coppicing* or *pollarding*.

Coppicing involved cutting a shrub or tree back down to ground level, then allowing it to grow again to produce a crop of small sticks or poles, depending on the age they were allowed to reach. Surprisingly enough, virtually all broadleaf trees respond to this treatment by remaining vigourous for centuries, or even thousands of years, rather than dying, and the practice was used for many generations to produce endless crops of wood materials. The most commonly coppiced trees are hazel, sweet chestnut, field maple, ash and oak.

Unfortunately coppiced trees produced shoots that were very good for deer or domestic animals to eat. Where animals could not be kept out, then pollarding was used – trees were cut off at above browsing height, and allowed to produce branches from there. The trees most often pollarded include beech, ash, willow and oak.

Keep an eye out for these different sorts of trees, and see if you can work out when they were last cut, or get an idea of how old the basic tree is.

How old is your wood?

Did you know that you can get a good idea of how old the wood you are looking at is? After the last ice age (about 18,000 years ago) most of western Europe was covered with forest, which has gradually been cleared away by man for settlement and agriculture. A few fragments of this original wood still exist here and there, although they are difficult to recognize. Most woods are actually *secondary*, meaning that they have grown up (or been planted) on land that was cleared of trees at one time. For example, in Britain there are many woods that look very ancient, but which have old field banks running through them, and so we know that they must have been cultivated fields in medieval or prehistoric times.

Maps provide the best starting point for working out the history of a wood. Try your library or public records office, and ask for the earliest maps of the area you are looking at. Is your wood there? Does it have the same shape, or was it larger or smaller? Sometimes, you will find that it is not shown at all, suggesting (but not proving) that it is more recent than the date of that map.

On the ground, try looking for clues that show the age of the wood. If the wood has banks around it, it is probably quite old. If they are narrow and well-defined, they are probably only one or two hundred years old, but if they are broad and spreading, they will be much older. Look for really old trees or tree stumps – the wood is probably older than the oldest trees in it. Some flowers only grow in ancient woodlands. Carpets of bluebells and wood sorrel are a wonderful feature of many southern woods. The keen eye may spot more unusual flowers like herb paris or early purple orchids amongst the display. Notice what flowers are there, and where they grow – you may find these 'old woodland' flowers only grow in one part of the wood, suggesting that the rest of the wood is much newer.

Wild garlic flourishes in damp clay soil at the edge of an ancient coppiced wood. This strong-smelling plant overpowers most of its neighbours.

A speckled wood butterfly, common throughout most of Europe, suns itself in a woodland glade.

THE ANNUAL CYCLE

If you have ever had to sweep up leaves in autumn you will know that trees shed a huge number of leaves each year. But in a woodland, with a dense canopy of trees shedding enormous quantities of leaves annually, no-one clears them up. So what happens to them? They become part of the natural system that operates in woods and supports so many species. A whole host of creatures, both plant and animal, feed on the rotting leaves and gradually break them down into simpler components. These creatures are known as *decomposers*, and they include fungi, bacteria, earthworms, springtail and millipedes. A square metre of woodland floor, to a depth of about 30 cm contains an incredible variety of life, all working away at the rotting leaves, fruit and wood. As the leaves are broken down, their components gradually become available again to the trees and other plants of the wood, and so the vital nutrient levels are kept stable.

Left: *A woodland floor in early autumn shows how quickly leaf litter can build up.*

Woodland fungi

In late summer and autumn, older woodlands are riddled with fungi (mushrooms and toadstools) as well as people collecting them. For the rest of the year, you hardly see any fungi, and then suddenly, there are masses. Where do they all come from?

As you might expect, fungi are present all through the year, even though you may not be able to see them. Below the fallen leaves, their growing stage, called a mycelium, digests the rotting leaf litter. The mycelium consists of a mass of white threads called hyphae, which can sometimes be seen if you turn over a fallen branch or some wet leaves.

At the end of the summer, and particularly after a wet period, the fungi produce their sporing bodies – the familiar mushrooms and toadstools. Toadstools come in all shapes, sizes and colours according to the species, but they all produce countless millions of spores. These are carried by the wind to a new part of the wood, where they grow into a new fungus.

Right: *The green-staining fungus tints the wood it grows on a blue-green colour. The stained wood is quite common but the cups are more infrequent.*

Far right: *The bracket fungus, Dryad's saddle, grows from a living ash stool in an ancient coppiced wood.*

PROJECT

Fungus spore prints

Toadstools are very common in woodlands, but they only last a few days before rotting away. Making a spore print will help to keep a record of them, as well as helping to identify them.

Select suitable specimens that have opened out, but not begun to go soft, then carefully cut the cap off, removing the stalk as close to the cap as possible. Now place the cap face down on a piece of white card (or try coloured card, if you find the spores are very pale). If you are working in a room that has any draughts, it is better to cover the cap with a bowl or something similar, otherwise the print will be distorted.

Whilst the cap is in position, it will be constantly shedding spores. These will fall directly onto the paper below (unless they are blown sideways) and will produce a clear print, if left for about 24 hours. The colour of the print, which varies from species to species, can help to identify your fungus.

If you want to keep the print, spray it lightly with art fixative spray, or some types of hairspray, but do not overspray. (*Always* follow the directions on the can – fixative sprays are *dangerous* if misused.) Label your print, if you know what it is, and keep it for future reference or display.

ANIMAL AND BIRD-LIFE

Birds depend on the structure of the wood and the shape of the trees in it. They make most use of woods in the breeding season, and a vast number of potential nesting sites are needed. Some birds nest in tree-holes, others high up in a fork, others on the ground; some like dense undergrowth, others prefer the site to be more open. Naturally enough, the more of these features that a wood can offer, the greater the variety of birds that will nest there. An old woodland, with a mixture of really ancient trees, will be absolutely full of nesting sites. Once birds start to rear their young, they then need a vast supply of food – almost all woodland birds rear their young on caterpillars, and the number and variety of these will depend on the species of trees present, with oak probably offering the best selection. So, next time you find a wood that seems to have a particularly good selection of birds, have a look at some of the features that might have made it suitable.

In addition to the birdlife, woodlands provide cover and food for a variety of mammals. Deer haunt the deep shade and cover, venturing out at dawn and dusk; look for their footprints in muddy tracks and trails. In the trees above, squirrels search for acorns and hazelnuts. These acrobatic animals are masters of the tree canopy, fearlessly leaping from branch to branch. Most of the seeds and nuts that the squirrels miss, fall to the ground, providing a rich harvest in the autumn for wood mice. These charming little mammals make their neat grass-lined nests among fallen branches and tree roots.

During the summer months, insects abound in the woodlands. Speckled wood butterflies haunt the glades whilst purple hair-streaks prefer the lofty heights of the leaf canopy. If you search amongst the leaf litter and fallen branches you are sure to come across many more insects. Beetles scurry for cover when exposed to the light, and slugs, snails and woodlice abound.

Top: *The nightingale is common enough in woods, but you are much more likely to hear one than see it as it is a very shy bird.*

Left: *A beautiful male pied flycatcher brings a hoverfly to its young in the nest hole, high in an old tree.*

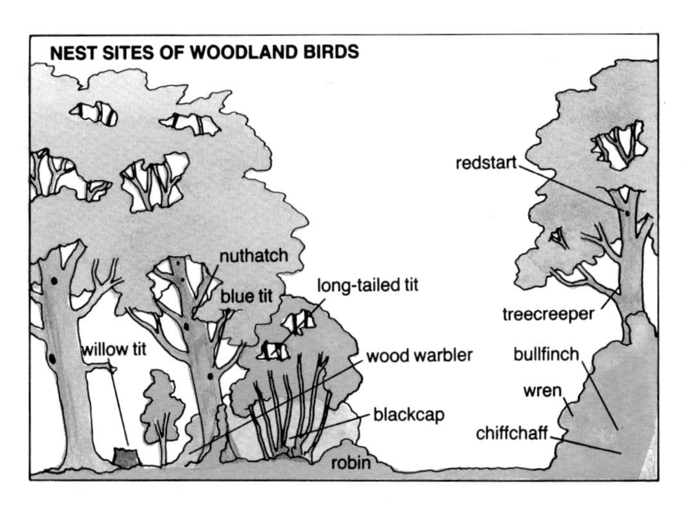

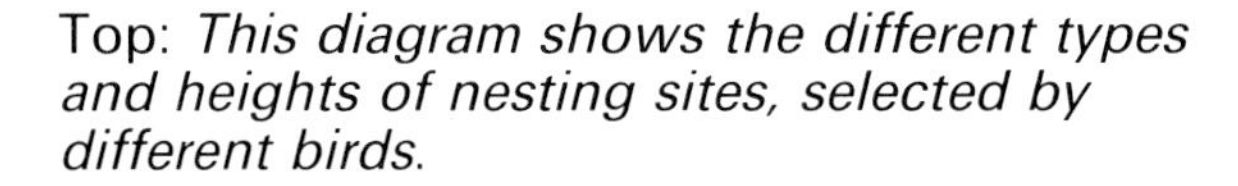

Top: *This diagram shows the different types and heights of nesting sites, selected by different birds.*

Right: Today, grey squirrels are a common sight in many woods.

Below: *At night, badgers forage for food on the forest floor. Earthworms are one of their main foods but their diet can vary enormously from season to season.*

GALLS

Have you ever noticed how some trees and bushes have odd-shaped deformities on them sometimes, like the red bushy 'robin's pincushions' on roses, or the hard spherical 'marble galls' on oaks? These are called galls, and they are almost always caused by some form of insect that lays its eggs into the tree or bush, and produces particular chemicals as it develops. These chemicals cause the plant to grow in a different way from usual, producing a well-formed protective 'house' for the young stages of the gall insect.

The life-cycles of some of these gall-causing insects are quite complicated, and they may sometimes form different galls at various stages of their life; for instance, one species of gall-wasp causes 'currant galls', that look like redcurrants, on oak flowers in spring, and 'spangle galls' on the undersides of oak leaves in autumn. If different insects come along and lay *their* eggs into the gall, their developing larvae will attack those of the gall-former – a further complication.

Nevertheless, you can still find out quite a bit about what is living in where by collecting a few fresh galls, and keeping them. Galls on leafy branches can be kept with the base of the branch in water, in a clear container, or fallen leaves can be kept moist in a box. Some time later, perhaps after several months, the insects will emerge, and these may be the original egg layers, or they may be something that has attacked and killed them.

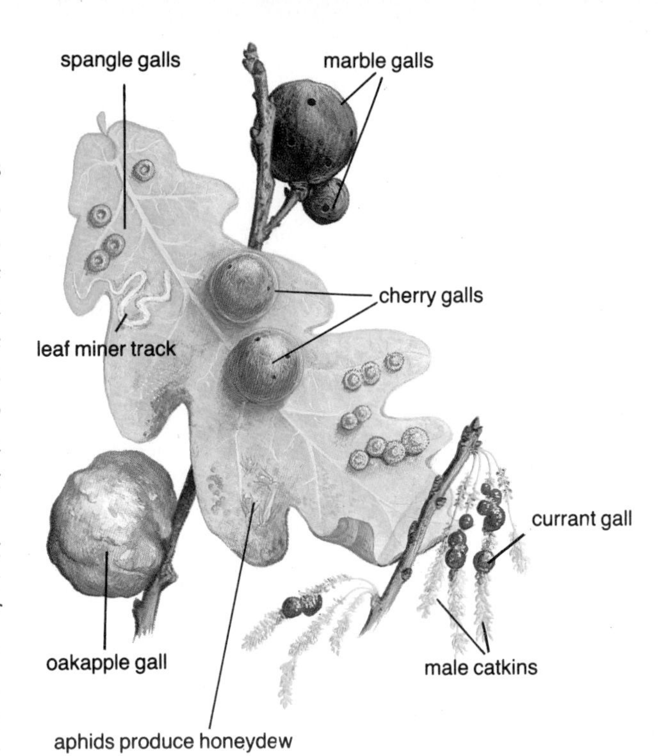

Left: *Strange-looking spangle galls are found on the underside of oak leaves.*

Above: *A green woodpecker arrives at its nest hole high in a forest tree.*

FUNGI AND FERNS

Hart's tongue fern
fronds up to 60 cm
Phyllitis scolopendrion. One of the most easily-recognized woodland ferns, because has quite undivided fronds, looking like a 'hart's tongue'. Underneath are lateral stripes which are the spore-producing bodies. Common in damp woodland.

Fly agaric
Amanita muscaria. Most distinctive of all woodland fungi, by virtue of bright red cap spotted with white. Usually grows under birches, less commonly under other trees, and fruiting bodies appear in autumn. Poisonous in large amounts.

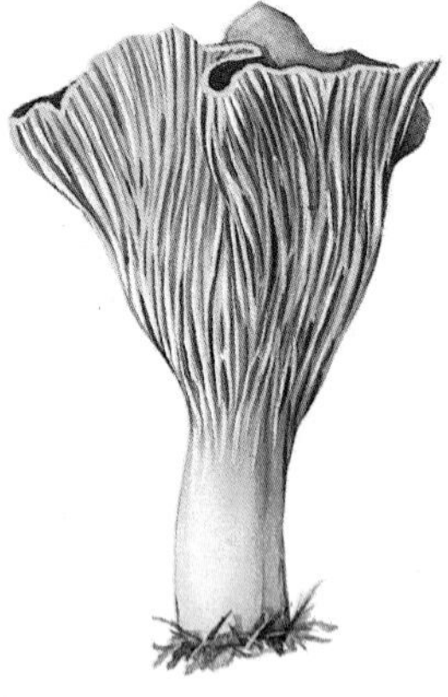

Chanterelle
Cantharellus cibarius. Familiar, but not very common fungus that grows in woods throughout Europe. Most commonly seen on market stalls, especially in France, as it is prized as delicacy to eat. Fruiting bodies usually appear in late summer or early autumn.

Male fern fronds up to 90 cm
Dryopteris filix-mas. Ferns are notoriously difficult to identify. This graceful fern grows in clumps, rather like a badminton shuttlecock. On undersides of fronds it produces heart-shaped reddish structures which bear spores. Many similar species have different-shaped spore bodies.

Stink-horn
Phallus impudicus. Strange-looking fungus, more often smelt than seen. Produces smell like rotting meat, to attract flies which feed on slime and carry fungus spores away with them. Spike emerges from structure looking rather like half-buried egg.

FLOWERS

Wood anemone ht 15–25 cm
Anemone nemorosa. Its beautiful white flowers are one of first signs of spring in woodlands, when they carpet ground in March. Flowers have marked rhythm, opening in day, and closing at night. Also known as wind flower.

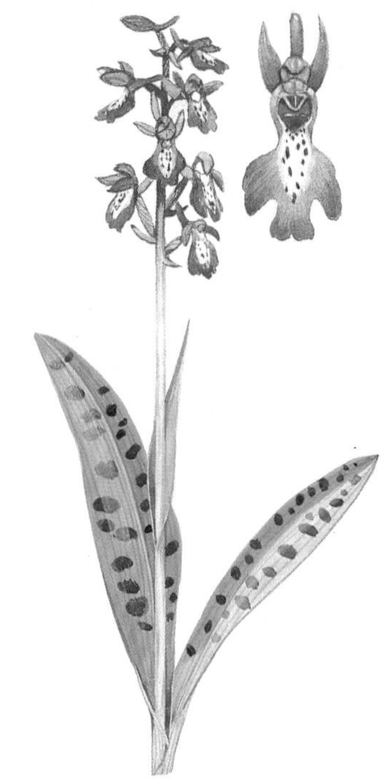

Early purple orchid ht 20–50 cm
Orchis mascula. Combination of deep red flowers and glossy purple-spotted leaves is attractive and distinctive. Flowers are pollinated by insects, which take away sticky mass of pollen whenever they visit a flower.

Primrose ht 5–12 cm
Primula vulgaris. The pale yellow flowers must be one of most familiar of all our wild flowers, and one of best-liked. Begins to flower as early as February, in sheltered spots, reaching a peak by April. Is still widespread, though less common than used to be, partly because people have dug plants up for their gardens.

Common dog violet ht 5–15 cm
Viola riviniana. One of a number of similar violets that can grow in woodland. Purplish flowers, hairless leaves, and white spur help to identify this particular one. Flowers in April and May normally, though there are sometimes more flowers in autumn.

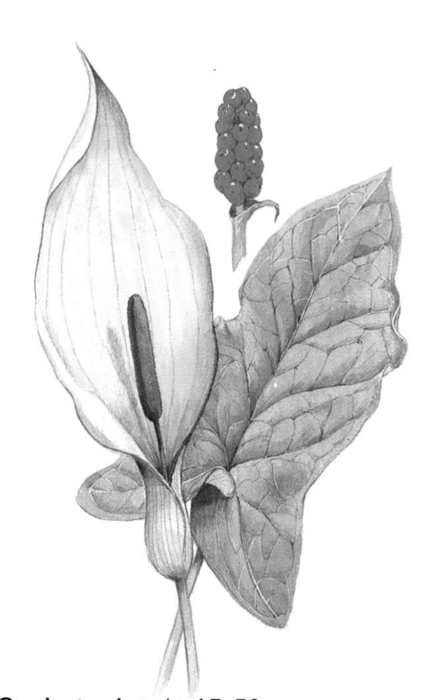

Cuckoo-pint ht 15–50 cm
Arum maculatum. Short plant, with large, dark green leaves, shaped like glossy arrowheads. Flowers very tiny, clustered on stalk and surrounded by pale green hood. Fruit bright scarlet and fleshy clustered at end of stalk.

Greater stitchwort ht 15–30 cm
Stellaria holostea. Grows in white frothy masses around edges of woodland, in clearings, and along hedges. Like most woodland flowers, it blooms in spring, reaching its peak in April and May.

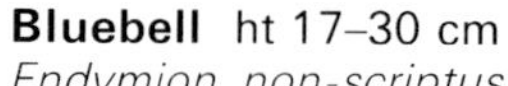

Bluebell ht 17–30 cm
Endymion non-scriptus. One of the wonders of woods in spring. Grows from bulb with smooth, narrow strap-shaped leaves. Flowers are small, bell-shaped, blue and occasionally white. Those in most gardens are bigger Spanish species in which flowering stem is erect, not drooping.

Bugle ht 15–30 cm
Ajuga vulgaris. Mauve-blue spikes of bugle flowers are common sight in damp woodlands, especially on calcareous soil. Plants creep around in grass, throwing up masses of spikes, which often carpet ground. Flowers, mainly produced in May, are very popular with insects.

Wild daffodil ht up to 35 cm
Narcissus pseudonarcissus. Much smaller than cultivated daffodil and is more delicate, with paler-coloured petals. Common in old-established woodlands, though rarely invades plantations. Flowers in March and April.

Ground ivy ht 15–60 cm
Glechoma hederacea. Low plant with creeping and rooting stems. Leaves heart-shaped with blunt-toothed edges. Flowers bluish-violet and narrow trumpet-shaped. Grows mainly on damp clay soil throughout most of Europe.

Foxglove ht 30–150 cm
Digitalis purpurea. The tall spires, with hanging purple 'gloves', are very distinctive. Occur in clearings in woods, or along edges. Biennial, flowering and dying in their second year, so constantly need to seed into new open areas.

Common oak ht up to 45 m
Quercus robus. It is one of two very similar species of oak in British woods. The other, Sessile oak, can be distinguished by unstalked acorns and long-stalked leaves. Both provide food, shelter and nest-sites for vast array of wildlife.

Silver birch ht up to 30 m
Betula pendula. Its familiar graceful form is common in woods on more acid soils. Short-lived (by tree standards) and less tall than other trees. Tends to colonize open areas quickly, but soon get shaded out by other more dominant trees.

Hazel ht up to 12 m
Corylus avellana. Usually an under shrub, though can grow into small tree. Has always been managed in past by coppicing (cutting back to ground level occasionally) so is usually seen as multi-stemmed shrub. Hazel nuts provide food for great range of birds and mammals every autumn.

Beech ht up to 40 m
Fagus sylvatica. One of the most elegant trees, with silvery bark, great height, and delicate branches. Widespread as native tree on both acid and chalk soils, and also widely planted in the past as its wood is excellent for making furniture.

Wych elm ht up to 40 m
Ulmus glabra. Can grow into an enormous tree when allowed to, though has often been coppiced or pollarded in the past. Leaves are very large in comparison to hedgerow elms, and does not produce suckers like most hedgerow elms. In early spring, little catkins are produced on the branches, long before leaves emerge.

Wild cherry ht up to 30 m
Prunus avium. One of our most beautiful native trees. In May, branches are covered by masses of large white flowers, just as bright green leaves unroll. The attractive red fruits are eaten by many birds and mammals, though are rather sour for humans. Also known as gean.

Holly ht up to 15 m
Ilex aquifolium. Occurs as woodland tree or shrub quite commonly, usually on acid soils. If growing in shade, rarely produces many berries. There are separate male and female bushes. Females only produce red berries.

INSECTS

Stag beetle bl 76 mm
Lucanus cervus. Male, with enlarged antlers, is one of our largest and most impressive insects, though quite harmless. Larvae live in dead wood, taking many years to mature, before eventually emerging to take flight in early summer. Females are smaller, without large antlers.

Brimstone butterfly
ws 52–60 mm
Gonepteryx rhamni. Original 'butter fly' (beautiful primrose yellow) but only males are yellow, while females are more creamy-white. Hibernates, and emerges early in spring, with a second generation in late summer.

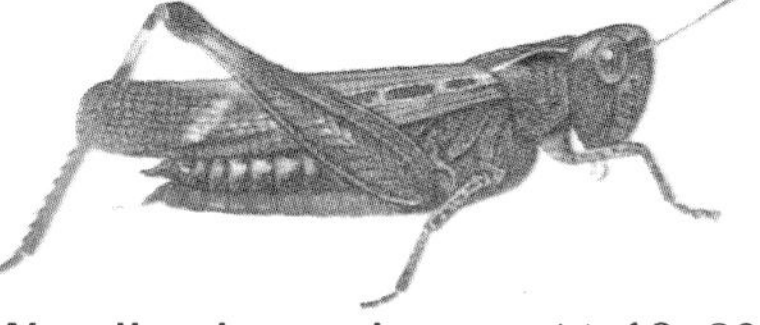

Woodland grasshopper bl 12–20 mm
Omocestus rufipes. Occurs in clearings and open areas in woods, where may be quite common. End of abdomen is often bright red, making it more conspicuous, but when insects keep still, they are almost impossible to see.

Speckled wood butterfly
ws 36–44 mm
Pararge aegeria. Most woodland butterflies prefer sunny glades and edges, but speckled wood is most at home in dappled shade of woodland interior. Common throughout western Europe, except far north, wherever there are suitable woodland habitats.

Silver-washed fritillary
ws 54–70 mm
Limenitis camilla. There are several woodland fritillary butterflies, but silver-washed is particularly large, and conspicuous by silvery underwings. Flies in high summer, and is most often seen at bramble and thistle flowers, feeding on nectar.

Red underwing moth
ws 65–75 mm
Catocala nupta. May look drab when at rest, but as it takes flight, bright red underwings 'flash', making it look quite different. This misleads predators, which lose sight of it when it settles again. Common in woodland and areas with trees.

Bee-fly ws 25 mm
Bombylius major. A furry bee-like fly commonly seen in spring in woods, visiting flowers such as primroses, where it sucks nectar through long proboscis. Hovers frequently, and may often feed while hovering, like tiny humming-bird. Larvae live in nests of bees and wasps.

Purple hairstreak ws 24–28 mm
Quercusia quercus. Only butterfly that actually feeds on oak trees in caterpillar stages, so, not surprisingly, is usually found in oak woodland. Not often seen, though, because spends much of its life around tops of trees, rarely coming down to flowers.

BIRDS

Tawny owl bl 38 cm
Strix aluco. One of our most familiar night birds, and originator of well-known 'tu-whit-tu-woo' calls. Harsher calls of young birds also a frequent feature of summer nights. Presence often detected by mobbing horde of small birds that often surround it in daytime.

Sparrowhawk bl 28–38 mm
Accipiter nisus. One of most common hawks in wooded country. Inconspicuous as it perches quietly in woodland, dashing out occasionally to chase a small bird with great agility. Female larger than the male.

Nuthatch bl 14 cm
Sitta europaea. Specialist in living in trees. Able to walk both up and down bark, looking for insect food in crevices. Much more beautiful close to than its pictures suggest. Nests in tree holes, that it may wall up with mud if too large.

Jay bl 34 cm
Garrulus glandarius. Common enough woodland bird throughout most of Europe, but often overlooked, due to its secretive habits. Feeds on almost anything, with particular fondness for acorns in season.

Redstart bl 14 cm
Phoenicurus phoenicurus. Widespread throughout most of Europe, wherever there are suitable old trees with nest holes. Both sexes have red tails, which they constantly flick (hence common name). Male more brightly coloured, with grey crown, white forehead, and black chin.

Woodcock bl 34 cm
Scolopax rusticola. Medium-sized bird, rather snipe-like in pictures, but very different in habits. Most often seen when 'roding' around its woodland territory in spring, at dusk, emitting strange assortment of noises.

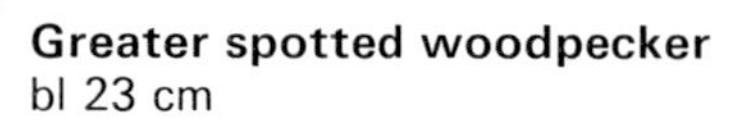

Greater spotted woodpecker bl 23 cm
Dendrocopos major. Common in older woodland, where there is plenty of dead and dying wood for making nest-holes in and prising invertebrate food out of. In spring courtship 'drumming' can be heard from surprising distance.

Pied flycatcher bl 13 cm
Ficedula hypoleuca. Nests in holes in old trees, usually in deciduous woodland, often close to running water. In Britain, only occurs in the west, where its habitat is more common. More widespread in mainland Europe.

MAMMALS

Beech marten bl up to 48 cm
Martes foina. A predatory mammal rather like a pine marten (*see p. 51*), but with pure white throat patch (not yellow). Occurs in deciduous woodlands throughout most of Europe.

Badger bl 61–76 cm
Meles meles. One of our most familiar mammals, from pictures, though rarely seen because of nocturnal and underground habits. Common in woods throughout most of Europe, living on variety of food. Earthworms are particular favourites.

Common dormouse bl 7.5 cm
Muscardinus avellanarius. The smallest of the dormice in Europe. Often also known as the hazel dormouse, because of liking for hazel bushes, and their nuts. Mainly active at night, but may occasionally be found sleeping in its nest.

Noctule bat ws up to 39 cm
Nyctalus noctula. One of our largest bats. Has distinctive dark yellowish-brown fur. Often one of the earliest bats to emerge – its ghostly silhouette may be seen fluttering around trees well before sunset.

Wood mouse bl 9 cm
Apodemus sylvaticus. Abundant throughout Britain and northern Europe, both in deciduous woods and other habitats. Also known as long-tailed field mouse. Like most small mammals, is nocturnal in habits, to try to avoid predators.

Grey squirrel bl 25.5 cm
Sciurus caroliniensis. Introduced North American species now common over most of lowland Britain, though not, as yet, in mainland Europe. Similar habits to the red squirrel, but much more common in deciduous woodlands. Tends to feed more often on the ground.

Wild boar ht at shoulder up to 1 m
Sus scrofa. Ancestor of the domestic pig, looks rather like a stocky, bristly pig. Piglets are striped cream and brown at first. Common through central Europe, wherever there is forest, but absent from UK and Scandinavia.

CONIFEROUS WOODLAND

Natural conifer woods are less common than deciduous woods in most parts of Europe. After the last great ice age, coniferous forests spread back into the tundra landscape more quickly than the deciduous forest, but as the climate changed they became more restricted and today the northern areas and mountains are where you are most likely to find natural coniferous forests. In Britain, for example, the only natural coniferous forests are in the highlands of Scotland, apart from a very few yew woods and juniper woods scattered through the country; and in France and Germany, you really have to go to the Alps or the Pyrenees to see the best coniferous forests.

However, it was discovered a long time ago that some conifers grow more quickly than most broadleaved trees, and can be planted to produce

A crested tit looks for food in a pine tree. This sedentary bird is recognized by its easily visible crest.

This natural pine wood is high in the Scottish mountains.

Above: *The straight lines of trees, all the same age, immediately show that this is a planted wood. The lines of trees are interrupted by wide fire-breaks. Spruces and pines grow well on poor upland soils.*

Right: *Diagram showing the development of a coniferous plantation. As the trees mature and cast more shade, there is progressively less chance of secondary growth beneath the branches.*

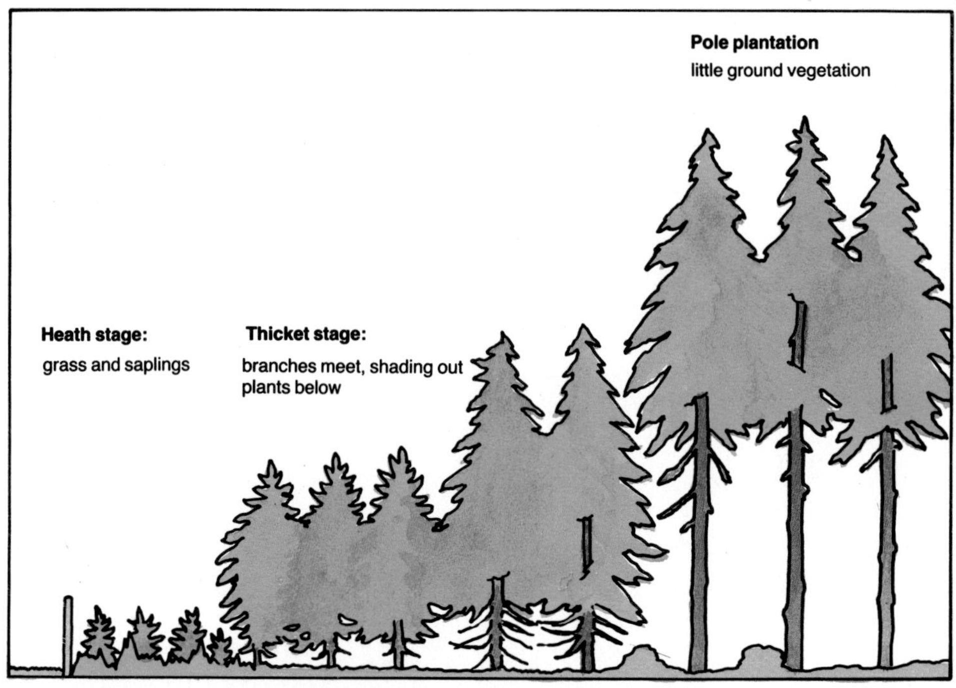

quite a quick crop (in terms of the normal life of trees) within 50 years or so. Some of the trees that are planted for this reason are already native plants of the area, such as the Norway spruce in many parts of Europe, or Scots pine, though others are imported from North America because they do particularly well in our climate, the Douglas firs, or Sitka spruce, for example. Conifers are planted today over large areas, and there are some huge forests, such as Kielder in Northumberland, England. This forest covers about 65,000 hectares of what used to be open moorland. It is now dense with conifers, all of them planted.

IS IT NATURAL OR PLANTED?

It is easy to confuse these two types of coniferous forest, and many people think that the only coniferous forests are those that are planted. However, they are just as different as an ancient oakwood and a new plantation of beech trees or eucalyptus. The plantations have dense rows of trees, all of the same age, with little variation in their shape, and no spaces in the canopy except where rides go through. The ground is usually ploughed and drained before planting, so it loses its natural variations, and because the land may not have been natural coniferous woodland before, none of the specialized conifer plants and animals occur there. In contrast, a natural conifer wood will have an interesting mixture of trees, some massive and very old, some medium-sized, and some young and small. There will be gaps, perhaps where a massive old tree has crashed down, or where the ground is too wet for trees to grow. There will be other trees, like birches or junipers, coming in here and there, and because the forest has probably been there for thousands of years, it supports the optimum number of plants, insects and animals.

Next time you go to a coniferous forest, have a look for some of these features, and see if you can work out whether it is planted or natural. It is usually easy to determine just by checking whether the trees are in rows and all the same age. Now and again you may be confused, either by a planted forest that is managed in a more interesting and varied way; or by a natural forest that is being managed commercially to produce something more like a plantation. If it is unclear just by looking at the trees, have a look at the woodland floor. The presence of many different flowers, such as chickweed wintergreen, may-lily, wintergreens and creeping ladies' tresses (see the identification guide), probably indicate that the wood is a natural one, whatever man has done to the trees.

Chickweed wintergreen growing in an old pine forest.

Which kind of wood do you think is the best for wildlife – the natural wood or the planted one? Not a difficult question; the natural ones are almost always much better. Sometimes plantations may provide suitable habitats for birds and animals while they are young, although a lot depends on what stage of growth these plantations are in.

LIFE IN CONIFER WOODS

Although conifer woods cannot really match the fantastic abundance of life in an established deciduous woodland, they are still marvellous places for the naturalist. They have many special features which you will not see in deciduous woods.

Above: *Although pines do not lose all their leaves in autumn, as do their deciduous counterparts, they do lose them gradually.*

Conifer woods differ quite fundamentally from their deciduous counterparts. They are more primitive than broadleaved trees, and they are also evergreen – that is they do not drop their leaves or needles all at once in autumn, but keep them all through the winter. Larch is the only conifer which is not evergreen. Plantlife in coniferous woods is affected by the constant shade. In deciduous woods, plants tend to flower before the tree comes into leaf, avoiding the dark summer period. In coniferous woods, there is no such difference, so the lightest time is simply midsummer, when the sun is highest in the sky and the days are longest. It is then that most coniferous wood plants flower, in June and July, without the tremendous synchronized display of the deciduous woods.

There is another difference, too. Most broadleaved trees and shrubs, like oak, ash and hazel, can be coppiced or pollarded, time and time again, to keep producing a supply of small wood. Conifer trees do not respond in this way, and if you cut them down to ground level, they simply die. Naturally enough, this has affected the way that man has used the woods, and in medieval times – before the days of pulpwood and paper-making – conifer woods had much less value. Ancient coppiced conifer woods are therefore not to be found and this is one reason why natural conifer woods have gradually become confined to the more inaccessible parts of Europe.

In deciduous woods, virtually all of the birds that breed there feed their offspring on caterpillars that appear in abundance on the young leaves. In coniferous woods, although there are many caterpillars, they are there in smaller numbers over a longer period. Because pines have tougher leaves and are less nutritious, the caterpillars take longer to grow, so they are of less use to the birds breeding at the normal time in spring. There is not enough food to support so many pairs of insect-eating birds, and the number and variety of such birds in conifer woods is therefore reduced.

There are, however, some birds that have

Below: *The beautiful and delicate flowers of the rare twinflower, growing amongst heather under pines.*

Above: *A crossbill, a characteristic bird of the coniferous zone, searching for seeds high up in a pine tree. A spruce-cone specialist, shortage of spruce seeds in some years causes it to migrate.*

adapted to conifer woods in different ways. The nutcracker, for example, is a large, attractive bird of the crow family, found in coniferous forests in the mountains of Europe and across northern Europe into Asia. It feeds almost exclusively on conifer seeds, especially those of pine, but it will also eat insects and other nuts and seeds if they are available. The crossbill is, perhaps, even more adapted for life in conifers – its whole food intake consists of conifer seeds, of various sorts, and even its young are fed on them. Its beak is especially adapted to prising seeds out of cones. It breeds very early in the year, starting in January or February, partly because conifer seeds are available right through the winter – unlike the caterpillars needed by most birds. But the young also grow more slowly on a seed diet than birds that live on caterpillars, so they need to start earlier.

The pine hawk moth is also to be found in conifer woods, the adult well camouflaged against the bark. The rare red squirrel and pine marten are also occasionally to be found.

A close view of a pine marten. This beautiful creature is becoming more rare, as its habitat is destroyed.

Making bark rubbings

A good way of making a reference collection of tree bark, without removing anything from the tree, is by making bark rubbings. These are fascinating and easy to make, and you will probably discover various things about the trees and their wildlife while you are making them.

You need some strong paper, not too thick, and preferably white, although other colours will do; some thick wax crayons, of any colour, and some string, pins, or blu-tack. Find a tree with suitable bark, which should not be too deeply cracked, nor heavily covered with lichens or mosses. Attach the paper using the string, pins, or blu-tack, to prevent it from moving while you are rubbing. Then carefully and smoothly rub the paper with the crayon, gradually transferring the bark pattern to the paper.

When you have finished, remove the paper, and identify it with a number or code, and then add any information about the tree to your notebook under that code. Remember to include the date, type of tree, approximate height or age and so on. Later, you can mount your rubbing, and write this information out neatly to go with it. You can gradually build up a useful and attractive collection, and you can even repeat some of them years later to see what changes have taken place.

Making casts from animal tracks

If you are observant, you will quite often see animal tracks in soft earth or mud. A few days after they are made, they will gradually become less distinct, and eventually disappear. However, you can actually keep them and take them home, by making plaster casts of them.

It is best to gather your materials together in advance. Carry them altogether in an old bag, so that you are instantly ready if you do find some good prints. You will need some strips of card about 30 cm long and 5–6 cm deep, with paper clips to make them into a circle; some plaster of paris, a bowl to mix it in, and an old spoon to mix it with; and some paper bags or old newspaper to put the damp casts into. You will also need water, or something to collect it in.

When you find some tracks, select the clearest, and make a card circle that will fit right round it without disturbing it. Push the card circle gently into the ground around the track. Now mix up enough plaster to fill the print. When it will just pour stiffly, carefully tip the plaster into the circle to a depth of about 2–3 cm, and leave it for about 15–20 minutes. By then it will be hard, but not totally dry. Meanwhile, you should wash the bowl out to prevent plaster from setting in that. Ease the whole thing out of the ground, including the mud below it, using a knife, trowel, or your spoon, and wrap it carefully in newspaper to carry home. After a few hours, it will have set really hard, and you can wash off the mud, remove the card, and generally clean it up.

A close look at insects

Although you will see a few insects of interest when you are just walking through a coniferous wood, or any other habitat, you will find out a lot more by delving a little more deeply. There are several ways that you can do this.

First, you can try making a beating tray. You need some light-coloured material stretched over a frame, or laid on the ground, and a solid stick. Select a suitable branch, place the tray or material below it, and give the branch one or two hard blows, enough to dislodge any resident insects, taking them by surprise. If you are lucky, all kinds of larvae, bugs, spiders, and so on will be shaken loose, and you will be able to get a really close look at them.

For insects and invertebrates in vegetation closer to the ground, it is best to use a sweep net, readily available from commercial suppliers. These are large nets which you sweep vigorously to and fro in the vegetation, and then empty to see what you have caught. The nets have to be strong to stand up to this treatment. For flying insects that you cannot get a good look at, such as dragonflies, or butterflies, it is best to use a smaller, more manoeuvrable butterfly net to catch them on the wing. When you have looked at them be sure to release them again.

It is also worth looking closely at tree-trunks, branches, and under leaves. Many creatures remain undetected simply by staying still. Several will be camouflaged, to look like their background or food plant, so look carefully.

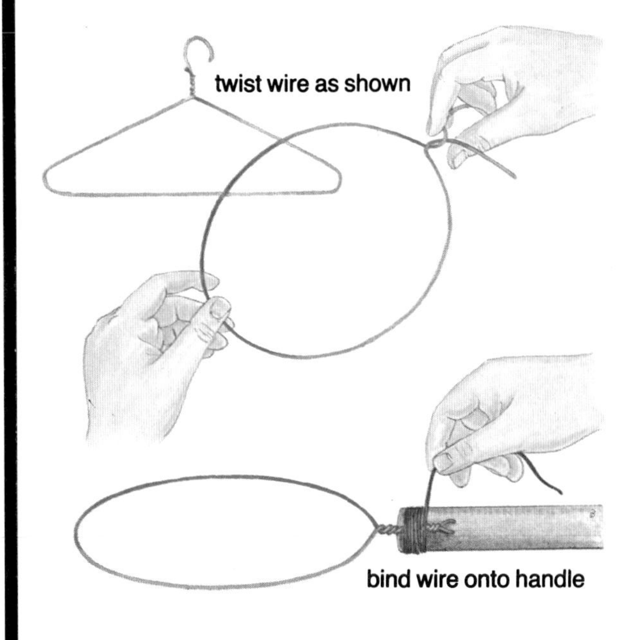

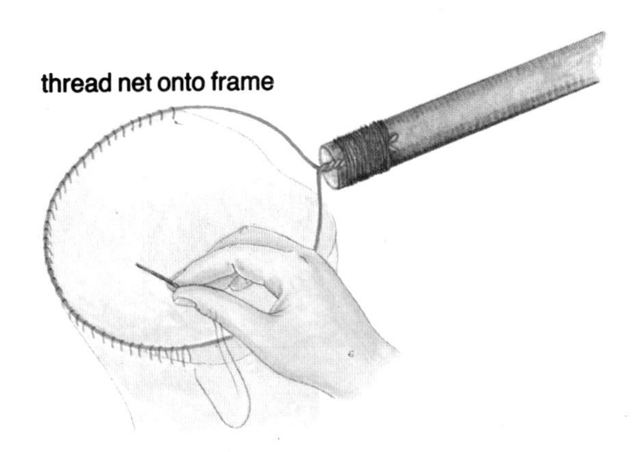

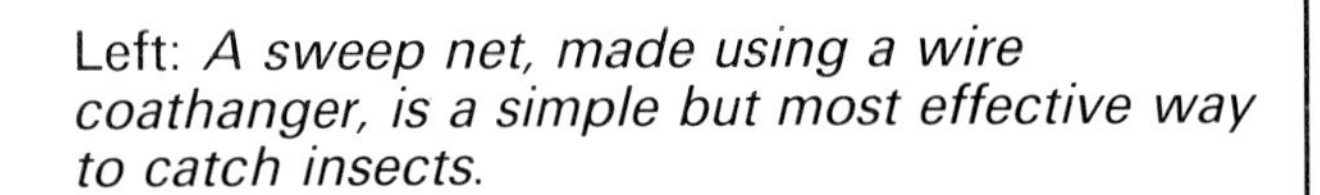
Left: *A sweep net, made using a wire coathanger, is a simple but most effective way to catch insects.*

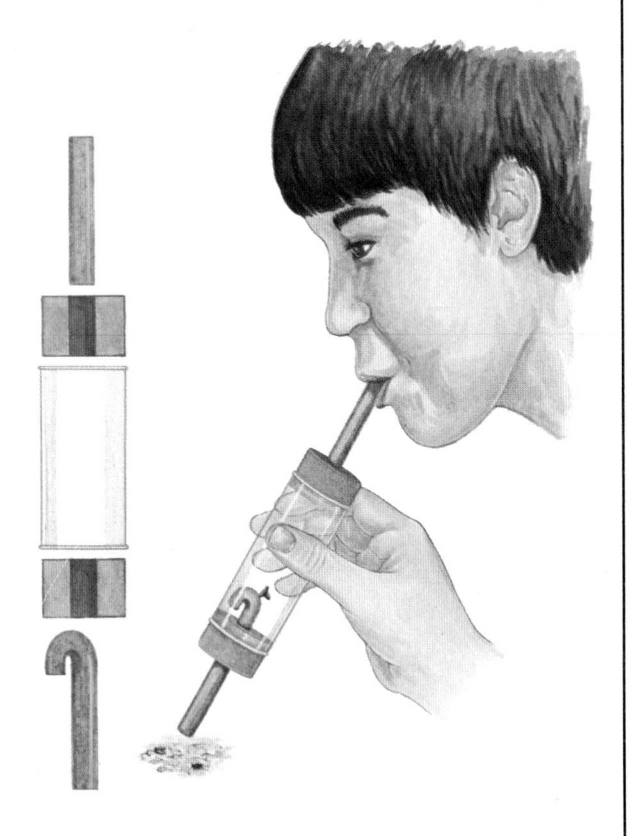

Above: *Many insects are too small to handle easily, and a simple pooter will enable you to pick them up without hurting them.*

Mammal watching

Coniferous forests are good places for watching mammals, and they are often easier to see than in deciduous forests. However, you must go well-prepared or you may be unsuccessful.

Wear dull-coloured clothing, and make sure that it does not rustle or make any other noises. If it is cold, wear plenty of layers, as it can be very cold just standing about, and wear suitable shoes that are quiet to walk in, but will keep you warm or dry if necessary. Take a pair of binoculars, a notebook and pencil, a map and something to eat.

The great thing to remember when mammal-watching is that mammals, unlike birds, have a very good sense of smell. They rely most on scent and hearing, and rather less on eyesight. This means

that you have to be sure to approach them upwind, with the wind blowing from them to you – unless you are in an area where they are very used to people, such as a park. As far as possible, always walk upwind, and whenever you come to a corner, or the brow of a hill, go around or over it very gently, trying to see anything there before it sees you. If you are approaching a likely spot, such as a grassy clearing or a drinking pond, go especially carefully. Always walk slowly and quietly when approaching mammals, or you will soon be noticed and you will never see anything.

If your quarry seems to have spotted you, stand absolutely still for a while. Unless you have been scented and heard as well, it will probably ignore you after a bit, and carry on feeding. However, once you have really been spotted, it is no good carrying on stalking the animal – it will just move away faster. A few smaller mammals, especially martens and weasels, may be curious about you, and if you see them go into a hole, it may be worth waiting a little to see if they re-emerge. Larger animals are unlikely to do this, however.

One final tip – the best time of day to go animal-watching is very early in the morning, so be prepared to get up at the crack of dawn. Remember, though, that it is always safer to go with a friend. The best time of year to see deer is often in autumn, when they are *rutting* (engaged in their mating and courting activities). They often get so engrossed that they are unlikely to see you or worry about you.

Left: *A beautiful red deer stag in his thick winter coat.*

Below: *A nimble red squirrel feeding on nuts in an old tree stump.*

FUNGI AND FERNS

Cep
Boletus edulis. Also called penny bun fungus, is one of most common and most-frequently eaten species of fungus, especially in mainland Europe. Large brownish caps often to be seen in markets in France and Germany.

The sickener
Russula emetica. Striking, attractive fungus but as name suggests, is very poisonous. Occurs commonly under pines, usually in autumn.

Hard fern ht 15–70 cm
Blechnum spicant. Small, rather inconspicuous fern. Grows in clumps and has different fronds for spores and for food production.

Broad buckler fern
fronds up to 60 cm
Dryopteris dilatata. Very common and widespread fern, both in coniferous woods and in other habitats. Although superficially like many other ferns, is more divided than most, and has distinctive golden scales, with brown stripe on the stems.

FLOWERS

Common wintergreen
ht 10–20 cm
Pyrola minor. Sends up short spikes of white or pinkish flowers in midsummer, from June to August. Widespread in coniferous woodlands and heathy areas throughout Britain and north Europe, though rarely very common.

Crowberry ht 30–50 cm
Empetrum nigrum. Prostrate, evergreen, mat-forming plant, that grows in open coniferous woodland or out on heather moors. Its small pink flowers are usually overlooked, but its large black berries (the 'crow' berry) are much more conspicuous.

Creeping ladies' tresses ht 20 cm
Goodyera repens. Surprisingly, one of the orchid family, with spirals of tiny white flowers twisted round stem. Look closely at individual flowers, which are very like some more exotic species of orchid.

Chickweed wintergreen
ht 10–20 cm
Trientalis europaea. Not related to chickweeds or wintergreens, but a member of primrose family (though pretty flowers look like anemones!). Frequent in conifer forests over much of Europe.

Bearberry ht 30–100 cm
Arctostaphylos uva-ursi. Low mat-forming shrub, that creeps around under trees, or on open moorland, producing clusters of pink flowers in early summer. Most common in northern or mountainous areas.

Norway spruce ht up to 65 m
Picea abies. Familiar Christmas tree of many countries, when cut young. Where native, forms forests of large graceful trees though is also widely planted as crop for timber production.

European larch ht 30–50 m
Larix decidua. Notable for beautiful fresh green foliage in spring: larches are the only deciduous conifers. Young cones are beautiful red colour at first, though become woody and brown later. Common in mountain forests, but not native in Britain.

Scots pine ht 25–35 m
Pinus sylvestris. Familiar and widespread conifer, notable for reddish flaking bark, and grey-green foliage of needles. Usually grow in open woodlands, with older trees having noticeable crown of branches at top, and few lower down.

Juniper ht up to 15 m
Juniperus communis. Small coniferous shrub or tree, with berry-like fruits or cones that eventually turn blue-black when mature. Fruits of juniper are used in gin making. Widespread as shrub below other conifers, occasionally forming woods on its own.

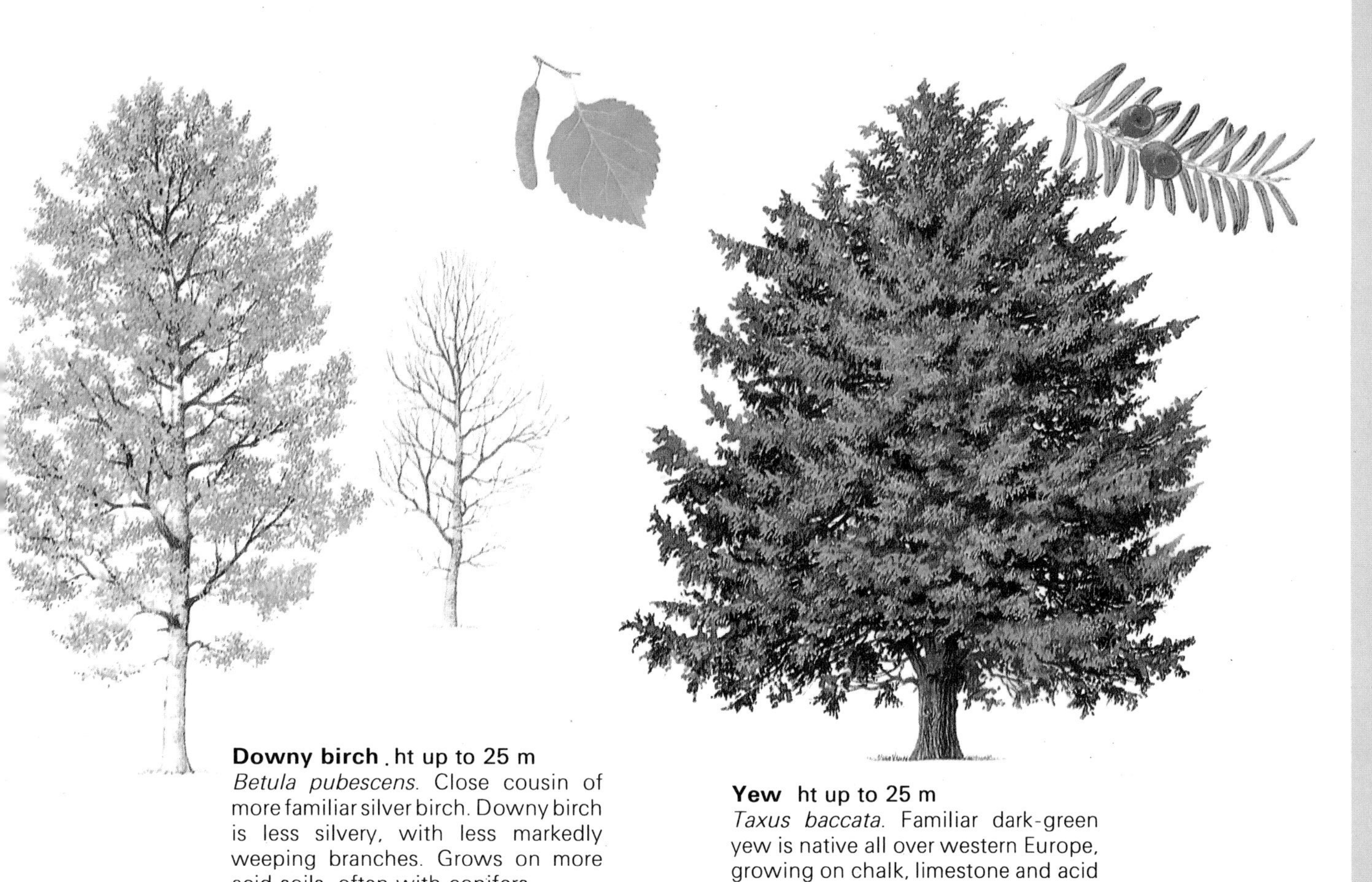

Downy birch ht up to 25 m
Betula pubescens. Close cousin of more familiar silver birch. Downy birch is less silvery, with less markedly weeping branches. Grows on more acid soils, often with conifers.

Yew ht up to 25 m
Taxus baccata. Familiar dark-green yew is native all over western Europe, growing on chalk, limestone and acid soils as well, often forming dense woods on its own. Also widely planted in churchyards, and some huge, and very ancient, specimens exist.

INSECTS

Pine hawkmoth ws 85 mm
Hyloicus pinastri. A large hawkmoth, whose caterpillars live on shoots of pines and spruces, throughout Europe. Grey-brown adults are well-camouflaged at rest on bark of conifers, so rarely seen in daytime.

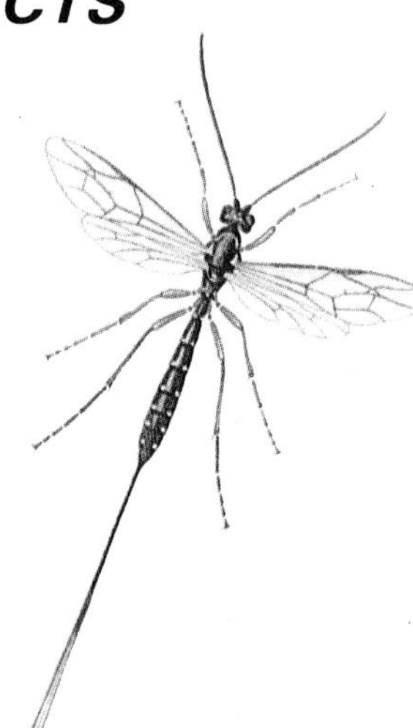

Horntail bl up to 37.5 mm
Urocerus gigas. Also called wood wasp. Actually is harmless sawfly, though it has appearance of a fearsome wasp. 'Tail' of female is actually an ovipositor, with which she bores hole in coniferous timber to lay her eggs in wood.

Ichneumon bl 35 mm
Rhyssa persuasoria. One of the largest of many ichneumons in Britain and Europe. Female's extraordinary 'tail' is actually an ovipositor, designed for boring into wood where larvae of horntail are living, as ichneumon parasitizes this species.

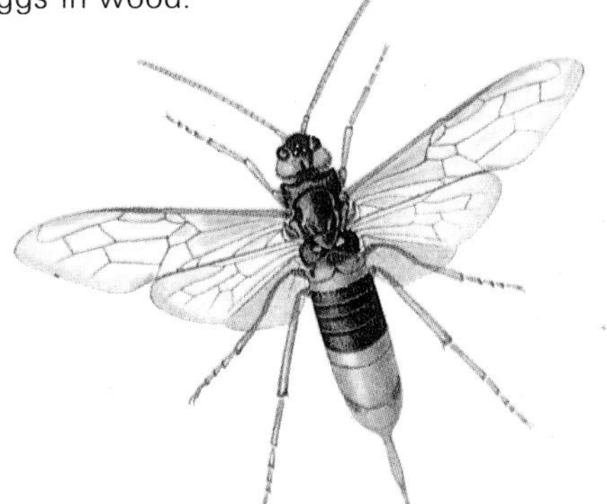

x3

Eyed ladybird bl 11 mm
Anatis ocellata. One of the largest and most distinctive of ladybirds, with yellow-ringed black spots. Like other ladybirds, feeds mainly on aphids, and is commonest in coniferous forests throughout western Europe.

Long-eared owl bl 36 cm
Asio otus. Medium-sized brown owl, with prominent ear-tufts (not actually the ears), giving it its common name. Occurs through most of Europe in coniferous woods, which can be huge forests, small copses or plantations, though never common.

Goshawk bl 48–60 cm
Accipiter gentilis. Rather like a large sparrowhawk, with same shape i.e. long tail, and short, rounded wings. Widespread through Europe, though never common, occurring particularly in large coniferous forests.

Capercaillie
bl 86 cm (male), 61 cm (female)
Tetrao urogallus. Enormous grouse-like bird, much larger than any related birds. Occurs scattered through Europe, usually in coniferous forests in mountain areas, including good population in Scotland.

Nutcracker bl 32 cm
Nucifraga caryocatactes. Rather untypical member of crow family. Has heavy, laboured flight, when short tail and rounded wings are very noticeable. Occurs in mainly coniferous forests, especially in mountain areas. Occasional immigrants reach Britain.

Cole tit bl 11.5 cm
Parus ater. Cole (or coal) tit is smallest of European tits. Most characteristic of conifer woods. Outside breeding season, mixed flocks of cole tits and other tits (and other small birds) join forces and range more widely in search of insect food.

Crested tit bl 11.5 cm
Parus cristatus. Readily distinguished from all other tits by prominent black-and-white crest on top of head. Almost always found in coniferous woods, especially pine, and is often to be seen among mature Scots pine. Widespread in mainland Europe.

Crossbill bl 16.5 cm
Loxia curvirostra. Strange-looking bird, probably the best adapted to life in conifers. Its crossed bill is particularly suited to extracting conifer seeds from cones, and it is dependent on these seeds all year round. Most frequent in spruce and fir forests, though it occurs in pinewoods in Scotland.

Goldcrest bl 9 cm
Regulus regulus. Along with firecrest, its close relative, this is Europe's smallest resident bird. Widespread throughout Europe especially in northern and mountain coniferous forests, though is more often detected by its high squeaking call rather than by being seen.

MAMMALS

Pine marten bl 42–52 cm
Martes martes. Attractive predatory animal, widespread through Europe, right to far north, in coniferous forests and mountain areas. In Britain, only occurs in more remote northern and western areas.

Fallow deer bl 1.75–2.5 m
Dama dama. Similar to red deer, but smaller. Reddish-brown coat in summer, with white spots. Coat greyer and spots less clear in winter. Male has branched antlers, wide and spade-like at top. Prefers open woodland and parks where can graze, as well as eat leaves of shrubs.

Red squirrel bl 20.5 cm
Sciurus vulgaris. Commonest squirrel over most of Europe, though in lowland Britain has largely been replaced by grey squirrel. Has a preference for coniferous woods, though occasionally also found in deciduous woods. Tends to stay in trees more than grey squirrel.

Roe deer bl 1–1.25 m
Capreolus capreolus. Smallest of more common species of deer. Widespread through most of Europe, except for far north and far south, occurring frequently in coniferous woodlands, though also in other habitats. Both males and females have sharp bark.

MEADOWS AND HEDGES

Meadows and hedges are storehouses of fascinating historical information and natural history. They are the product of man's efforts, over thousands of years, to clear the land of natural forest and create agricultural land to live by.

At first, meadows were just simple clearings in the forest, but as the size and number of clearings grew, there was a need to be better organized. For example, where two adjacent families enlarged their own clearings until they met, something had to be used to indicate the boundary, and the answer in this case was often to leave a strip of the original forest. Similarly, as the amount of cleared land grew larger, so it became necessary to subdivide it in order to keep grazing animals off

Much of the countryside, especially in hill regions, is made up of a mixture of meadows and hedges where adonis blue butterflies (left) can be seen. This butterfly has been the subject of conservation projects which have successfully increased its numbers.

the crops, and so on. So gradually, we ended up with the patchwork landscape that is the hallmark of our more historic countryside. Unfortunately, the process has continued much too far in areas where the soil is fertile or easy to work. As a result, the fields have become huge, and the hedges have disappeared altogether.

MEADOWS AND PASTURES – THE DIFFERENCE

Meadows are no more natural than the hedges that surround them. You may have noticed that, if a piece of grassy land is left abandoned, it first becomes rough and tussocky, then bushes start to appear, and then finally birches, alders, ash trees, and ultimately oaks will invade it. If left to its own devices, it will eventually just become a woodland again, and, in fact, many woods in the countryside have arisen in just this way. In other words, meadows and pastures only remain as grassland if we continue to manage them.

There is actually a slight difference between meadows and pastures, according to how they are managed – meadows are cut for hay, while pastures are grazed. Try looking at a piece of grassland, and working out whether it is pasture or meadow. It is easy if there are animals grazing it, or someone is mowing it for hay, but what if there is neither there when you see it?

A meadow in chalk downland in summer full of wild flowers.

Hedges have originated in three ways: some evolved naturally along boundaries of unused land; some are the remains of woodland, left when fields were cleared on each side and some were planted.

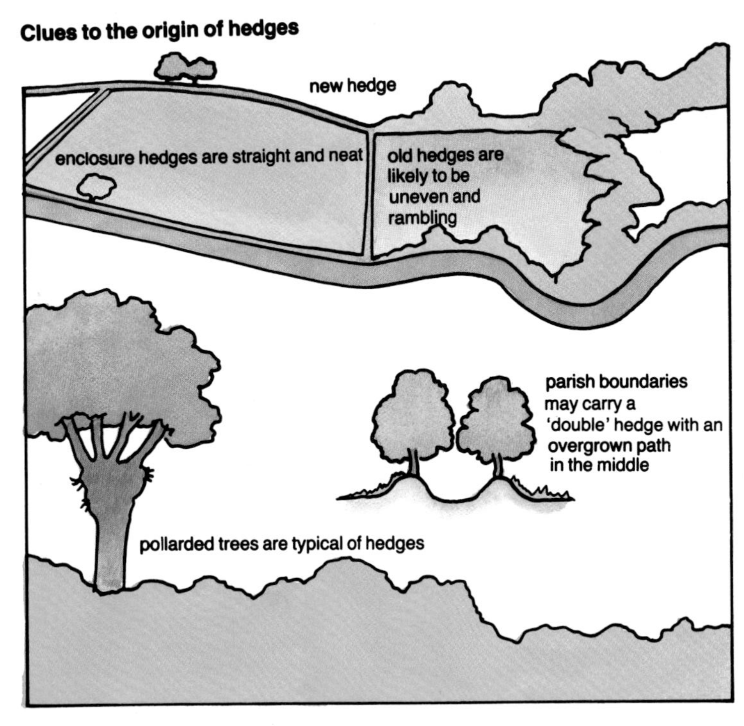

Actually, it is not quite as difficult as it seems, and there are some clues you can look for:

- Meadows are usually fairly flat, regularly-shaped and not too marshy. If they were too steep, uneven, irregular in shape, or wet, they could not be mown.
- Pastures are often on land that is not used for anything else, so they include steep banks, uneven or rocky ground, wet ground, and so on.
- If you see lots of grassy hummocks in a field, about 30–40 cm high, and a little more across, these will almost certainly be anthills, built by meadow ants. They take a long time to develop to this size, and if there are quite a few reasonably large ones, you can be pretty sure that you are looking at a pasture, because anthills and mowing do not mix! You can also be pretty sure that the pasture has not been ploughed for 100 years or more, because ploughing destroys the anthills. Unbelievably, some species of ant need 200 undisturbed years to enable large colonies to develop.

LIFE IN A MEADOW

The wildlife of a meadow depends on how it is managed. Meadows are not three-dimensional, as a woodland is, and their ecology is much more simple. The plants, for example, must be able to survive being cut back every year, or grazed most of the time, so they tend to be perennial (long-lived) plants that can survive close to ground level, and reproduce themselves by sending out shoots, rather than by having to produce seeds. Insects have to be able to adapt to management, too. For example, butterflies tend not to do very well in meadows that are cut back each year for hay, because all their food plants and nectar sources are removed at a stroke. Grazed pastures, especially on chalky soils, are very attractive to butterflies, though, as their caterpillar food plants occur there. The caterpillars adapt to living under grazed conditions by feeding mainly at night and retreating to the bases of the plants by day.

Meadows can have a great deal to offer mammals, but much depends on the length of the grass. In very short grass, such as sheep-grazed pasture, or regularly-mown grass, there are very few mammals, because there is nowhere for them to hide. You may see rabbits if there is some cover for them nearby, and hares will be there if the area is large enough to allow them to see any danger and run away from it, but there will be virtually no mice or voles. In rather longer grass, that is only cut occasionally, or just lightly grazed by cattle, there will be masses of small mammals such as mice, voles, and shrews, and probably a few larger ones such as weasels or stoats that hunt out the small mammals for food. The soil underneath provides a home for one specially equipped mammal – the mole. The velvet-covered mole lives virtually all its life underground, except on occasional rainy nights when it comes up for earthworms, and it is particularly abundant in grasslands.

Some birds specialize in nesting in meadows, especially damp ones where there is more food for their developing young. There is a marked difference, though, between the birds of mown hay meadows and those of grazed pastures. Very few birds breed in hay meadows, unless the hay is cut very late, because they cannot complete their breeding cycle before the cutting starts, and because the even height of vegetation can make it difficult for them to re-find their nests.

In tussocky pastures you will find breeding redshank, snipe, yellow wagtail, lapwings, and maybe godwits or curlews. In winter, many birds gather on grasslands to feed on the seeds of the meadow plants or to probe into the soil for invertebrates like the vast flocks of rooks, starlings, or lapwings, do.

LIFE IN A HEDGE

Hedgerows harbour the same sort of species that you might find on the edge of woodland. Birds and mammals make use of the cover provided and insects visit the hedgerow flowers to feast on the nectar.

During the spring, up to ten different species of bird nest in our hedgerows. Yellowhammers, easily recognized by their yellow plumage and jingling song, build neat little nests high in the branches. Dunnocks and bullfinches build lower down, and search for caterpillars and spiders to feed their young. At ground level, pheasants and partridges rely on their camouflage to avoid detection.

In the autumn, hedgerows provide a harvest of fruit and berries for wildlife. Tiny harvest mice scour the branches for blackberries, competing with migrant birds for these juicy morsels. Comma butterflies collect nectar from the flowers, and bush crickets chirp in the undergrowth.

WORKING OUT THE AGE OF A HEDGE

Hedges can be almost any age. They may have been newly planted or be a strip left from the original natural woodland, when the land was first being cleared thousands of years ago. In practice, of course, most of them are somewhere in between, and it is common for the hedges within an area to vary from 100 years old to about 1000 years old. It is difficult to find reliable maps of how things were more than about 200 years ago (though there are a few, for some areas), so how can you work out the age of the hedges in your area? Surprisingly, it is possible, just by using the plants that grow there.

Some years ago, an ecologist discovered that the number of species of trees and shrubs in a hedge increased with the age of the hedge. He also found that there was a definite relationship, which was that approximately one extra species developed every 100 years. He showed that, if you count the number of species of woody plants in a 30 metre stretch of hedge, then multiply your answer by 100, you will get an idea of the age of the hedge in years. For example, if you found three species in a hedge, it would probably be about 300 years old.

When doing this calculation, there are a few things to take note of:

- Don't worry too much about precisely identifying each species – collect a leaf of those that you do

Left: *An old anthill on chalk downland has been covered with wild thyme.*

Right: *A lovely view of meadow countryside at haymaking time. This field is a mixture of arable and grazing land.*

not know, and just count up each new species, whatever it is.

- Include roses, but ignore brambles and woody climbers, such as old man's beard and honeysuckle.
- It is best if you can count several separate stretches, and average the results, to avoid the possibility of a chance high or low result.
- Do not expect complete accuracy. The method's accuracy varies from one area to another, because of the effect of climate and different history, so if you can check any of your results against maps or documents, you may find you need to adjust your calculation a bit.

Whenever you are looking at hedges, take note of other features, such as whether the shrubs are growing on a bank (this tends to show an older hedge). Look on the map to see if the hedge runs along a parish or other boundary – very often these are the oldest hedges in an area.

Above: *A mass of flowers in a mature banked hedge in Cornwall. Goosegrass abounds with foxgloves, red valerian and cow parsley in the foreground.*

Left: *This carefully controlled roadside verge and hedgerow is a haven for wildlife.*

Looking at spiders' webs

Hedges and uncut grasslands are excellent places for seeing spiders' webs. Not all spiders make webs, some species hunt their prey by other means. But a lot of different spiders do use webs, and they are one of the few groups of animals that set traps for their prey.

If you visit a hedgerow in autumn, especially on a misty morning, you will see literally dozens of spiders' webs. Most of these will be occupied, so just imagine how many spiders are present! The purpose of these webs is to catch insects that are flying past. The spider then pounces on and immediately immobilizes the trapped insect with poison and silk.

If you look carefully, you will see that there are many different sorts of webs. Perhaps the most familiar are the big orb-webs, constructed in a roughly circular shape, with silken threads radiating out from the middle and attaching them to the vegetation. The spider most usually responsible for these in most of north-west Europe, is the orb-web spider or garden spider, with a large white cross on her back. You may also see the very abundant webs of the money spiders; these are built parallel to the ground, and are rather like little hammocks, made of a dense network of threads. Someone once worked out that you may find up to three million of these webs in one hectare of suitable land!

The silk produced by spiders is incredibly strong, with more breaking power than steel for the equivalent thickness of thread. Have a look at a few webs and try to work out how they are constructed and attached to the vegetation. Attempting to draw their patterns is very revealing – you see just where the strands go. Have a look at the contents of the web, too, and see if you can work out what has been caught. Occasionally, you will come across scavengers who have learnt to avoid detection by the resident spider, creeping across the web to eat the contents; the strangely-shaped scorpion fly is a good example.

Right: *A female garden spider waits at the centre of its circular orb-web for an unsuspecting victim.*

Left: *A beautiful young red fox emerges cautiously from the undergrowth.*

Below: *A lapwing, easily recognized by its long, thin crest and broad rounded wings, settles on its nest with three eggs in a damp meadow.*

Left: *A group of rabbits, alert for possible predators, graze in a meadow in the early morning.*

Far left: *A close view of a grasshopper resting on a hawk-bit flower.*

Animal tracks, trails and signs

You may be frustrated by the fleeting glimpses you get of some of our more secretive animals like deer, squirrels and owls. However, with a bit of know-how you can become a nature detective and piece together the secret lives of our wildlife.

Deer are generally shy animals which prefer to remain concealed in the woodland shade by day. However, by night they venture out into the open, often using well-trodden trails. Where soft mud collects along these woodland rides, you will find their footprints, which are known as 'slots'. By careful observation you can tell which species of deer have made the prints and even how many individuals are involved. Try making a plaster-cast of the prints as a permanent record.

Many of our small mammals feast on the autumn's abundance of nuts. Hazelnuts and acorns both have hard cases which the mice and voles have to nibble through to reach their reward. Since each species nibbles in a very different way you can tell who has been at work. Dormice make perfectly smooth, round holes whereas wood mice tear jagged edges, making obvious tooth-marks.

Rabbits, rats, foxes and badgers all live in burrows. Here they spend most of the day in snug dens waiting for nightfall. Not all burrows are occupied and to tell whether any creature is in residence, look for smooth soils around the entrance and signs of bedding material. To be completely certain, place a blade of grass across the entrance to see whether it is dislodged by the owner's exit.

Birds also leave tell-tale signs which help to reveal their lives. Water birds leave their footprints in the muddy margins of ponds and lakes and many produce characteristic droppings. Red grouse, for example, produce piles of droppings which look exactly like cigarette ash. These are left in hollows in the moorland heather and close by you may also find their dust baths, surrounded by down feathers. Birds also regurgitate the indigestible part of their food as pellets. By dissecting these you can find what the bird has been eating.

Above: *Hazelnuts wedged into crevices in tree bark and opened by nuthatches, leave a regular rounded hole.*

Below left: *A badger footprint in wet mud. Claws and pads are clearly defined.*

Below: *A selection of food remains show feeding signs.*

Inspecting bird pellets

Most birds, when they eat, take in a lot of material that they cannot digest, and many of them regurgitate the least digestible parts of their diet as pellets. Although many small birds produce pellets, you are more likely to find large pellets from birds of prey or owls. These make interesting subjects for study, because you can find out just what a bird has been eating – something that it would be very difficult to do otherwise.

Although the pellets are soft and slimy when first regurgitated, they soon become dry and clean to handle. You may find pellets almost anywhere in the countryside, but you can also try searching in old barns, under large trees, by old fence posts, and anywhere that you know owls, kestrels, or other birds of prey may perch. If you have seen a particular bird in the place where the pellet was found, this will help to identify the pellet; on the other hand you can easily work out what kind of pellet it is from reference books, as each species produces pellets of a different shape and colour.

At home, you can take the pellet apart, to see what is in it. It is best to soak the pellet in water for a few hours, removing any loose material and dirt in the water, then rinsing the contents again, shaking the jar gently. After this, it is easy to pick out any items of interest with a pair of fine tweezers or a dissecting needle. Alternatively, you can take the pellet apart dry, but this is much more difficult. It is possible to identify many of the bones you find, and they can be kept as an interesting collection if cleaned and bleached.

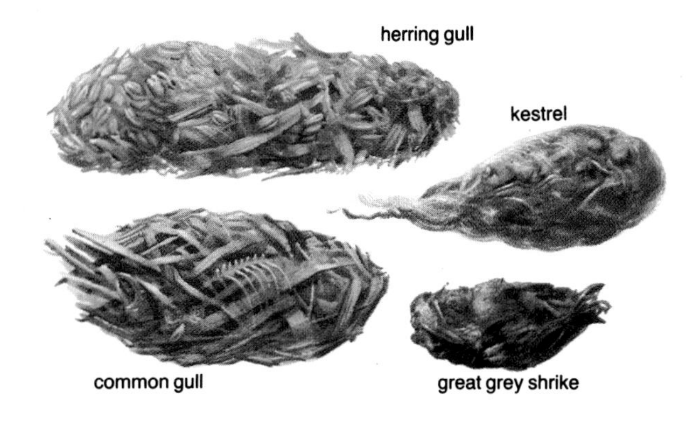

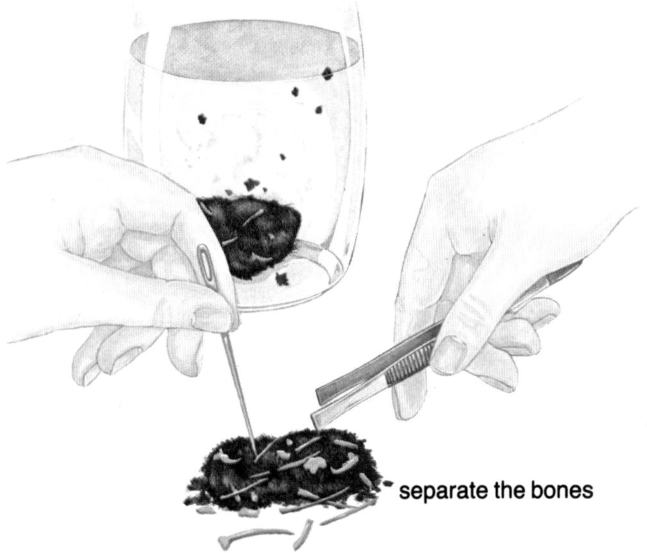

Below: *The pellet of a buzzard with the fur and bones of small mammals clearly visible.*

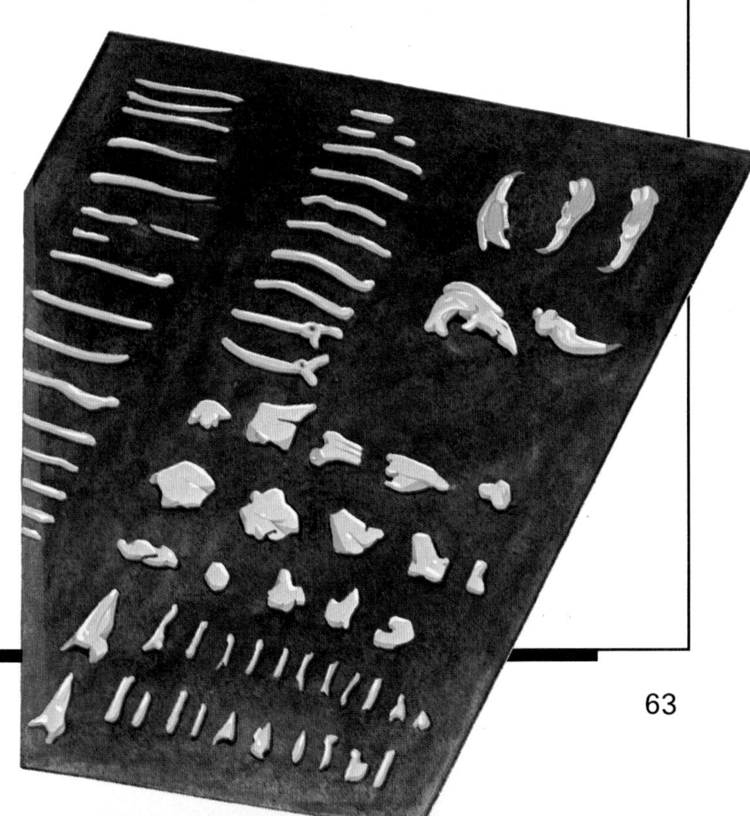

FUNGI AND FERNS

Adders tongue fern
Ophioglossum vulgare. Plant of old meadows, where its creeping root system allows it to spread. Looks unlike most other ferns, but still produces typical fern spores in spike-like structure in early summer.

Parasol mushroom
Lepiota procera. Large and very distinctive toadstool. Widespread in meadows and pastures, though rarely common, and excellent to eat. Most frequently seen in late summer and autumn.

Shaggy ink-cap
Coprinus comatus. Strange fungus emerging from ground white, but rapidly turning to inky black as cap dissolves with age. Also called Lawyer's wig, referring to way cap gradually breaks up, looking rather like curly wig.

Field mushroom
Agaricus campestris. Probably most common and best-known of wild mushrooms, appearing in late summer and autumn, especially after rain, in rich pastureland. Edible and particularly palatable.

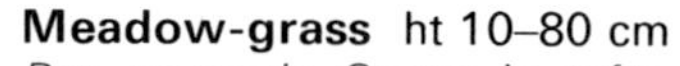

FLOWERS

Meadow-grass ht 10–80 cm
Poa pratensis. Grows in tufts, with slender, creeping stems. Flowering stems tall with groups of very thin branches growing out from near top. Each branch has small, flat group of flowers at end, which, as in all grasses, have no coloured petals. Do not look, therefore, like 'flowers'.

Cow parsley ht 70–130 mm
Anthriscus sylvestris. One of the many similar plants bearing umbels ('umbrellas') of white flowers. Flowers often so abundant along hedgerows in May that they completely colour the hedge-bottom white for a while.

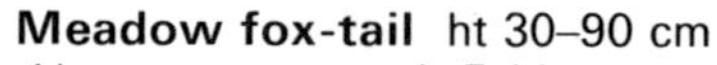

Meadow fox-tail ht 30–90 cm
Alopecurus pratensis. Fairly easy grass to recognize. Flowers make mass, near upper stem. Each flower has short, stiff hair which sticks out and these make whole mass look like hairy fox tail.

Cocksfoot ht up to 1.5 m
Dactylis glomerata. Coarse grass that grows in tufts with rough leaves. Thin, stiff stems. Flowers in tight groups at end. So called because flower groups have shape of cock's foot. Also found by roadsides.

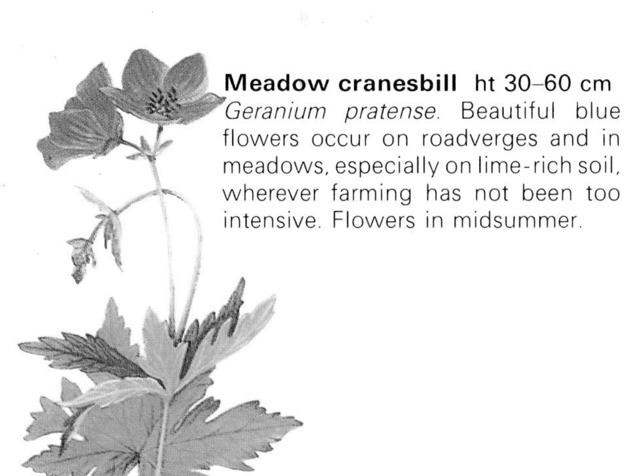

Meadow cranesbill ht 30–60 cm
Geranium pratense. Beautiful blue flowers occur on roadverges and in meadows, especially on lime-rich soil, wherever farming has not been too intensive. Flowers in midsummer.

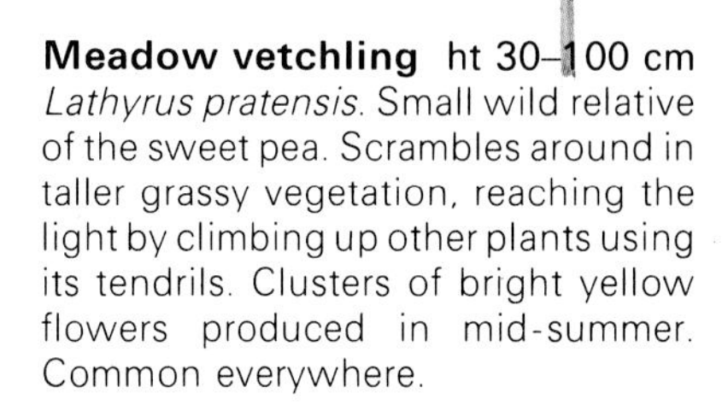

Meadow vetchling ht 30–100 cm
Lathyrus pratensis. Small wild relative of the sweet pea. Scrambles around in taller grassy vegetation, reaching the light by climbing up other plants using its tendrils. Clusters of bright yellow flowers produced in mid-summer. Common everywhere.

Red campion ht up to 80 cm
Lychnis dioica. Great feature of hedges, verges and woodland edges in early summer. There are separate male and female plants, though you have to look hard to spot differences. Only the female plants produce any seeds.

Sweet violet ht 1–10 cm
Viola odorata. Flowers in early spring along hedges and lanes, and comes in two colours – blue or white. Has large heart-shaped leaves, and flowers really do smell sweet, unlike most other violets.

TREES AND SHRUBS

Blackthorn ht up to 6 m
Prunus spinosa. Frequent hedgerow plant everywhere, with characteristic habit of producing masses of white flowers before the leaves come out in spring (unlike hawthorn). Later, produces masses of blue-black sloes, like small damsons.

Spindle ht up to 6 m
Euonymus europaeus. For much of year rather dull, dark green bush, with barely-noticeable flowers. Comes into its own in autumn when orange berries protrude from pinky-purple fleshy surrounds. Common on chalky soils.

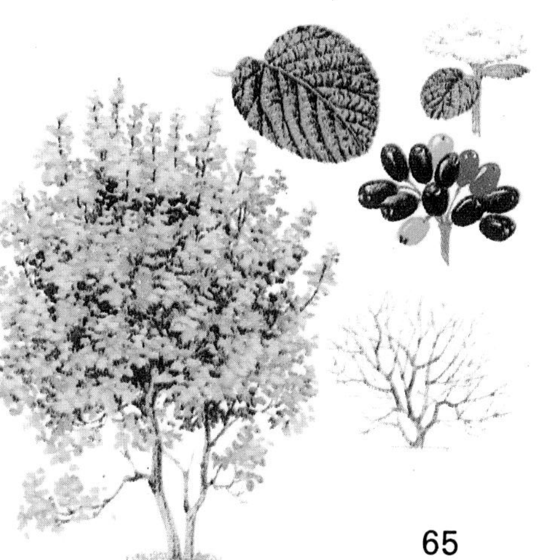

Wayfaring tree ht up to 6 m
Viburnum lantana. Widespread and often very common in hedges, wood edges and scrub on chalky soils throughout Europe. Flowers in April and May, followed by red berries that gradually turn black.

Field maple ht up to 20 m
Acer campestre. Forms large shrub or small tree, up to about 20 m high in favourable conditions. Most common on chalky or clay soils, and becomes particularly distinctive when leaves turn golden yellow in autumn.

Ash ht up to 40 m
Fraxinus excelsior. Grey bark and black buds of ash are familiar features of countryside, where it occurs in hedges, amongst scrub, and elsewhere, with particular liking for limey soils. Always one of last trees to come into leaf, often remaining bare until late May.

Hawthorn ht up to 10 m
Crataegus monogyna. Also called may. Common and familiar shrub or small tree, growing to a height of 10 m if undisturbed. In May, produces frothy pungent-smelling blossom, followed by red haws in late summer and autumn.

Rowan ht up to 20 m
Sorbus aucuparia. Combination of 'plates' of creamy-white flowers in spring, bright red berries in summer, and beautiful divided leaves very attractive, and easily recognizable. Common throughout Europe, especially where soil is acid.

Sallow ht 3–10 m
Salix capraea. Member of the willow family, and, like most willows, produces male 'pussy willow' catkins in spring. Later in year, female flowers produce fluffy seeds that disperse widely in wind. Grows to about 10 metres, forming a shrub or small tree.

INSECTS AND OTHER INVERTEBRATES

Common blue ws 28–36 mm
Polyommatus icarus. There are several species of blues. Common most likely to be seen in large numbers in meadows. Male is handsome pale blue, but female dull brown with spots. Slug-like caterpillars feed on low-growing herbs, such as bird's foot trefoil and clover.

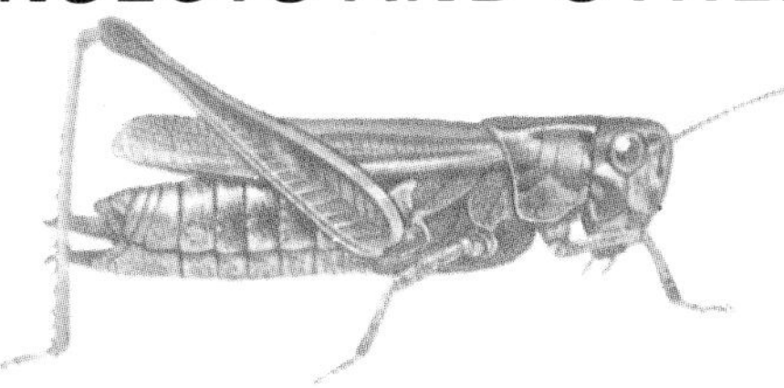

Green grasshopper bl 20 mm
Omacestus viridulus. Found in grassy places and heard throughout summer months over most of Europe. Hard to see because of green and brown colour. Also found in woodland clearings and roadside verges. Feeds on grasses and other low-growing plants.

Brown-lipped snail bl 20 mm
Cepaea nemoralis. One of several common banded snails, to be found all over Europe in suitable habitats, especially where soil contains lime which helps shell formation. Almost always has brown lip, which helps to identify it.

Meadow brown ws 44–50 mm
Maniola jurtina. One of most abundant of all summer butterflies, often occurring in clouds over longer grass areas. Caterpillars feed on grasses, so is particularly suited to meadow habitat.

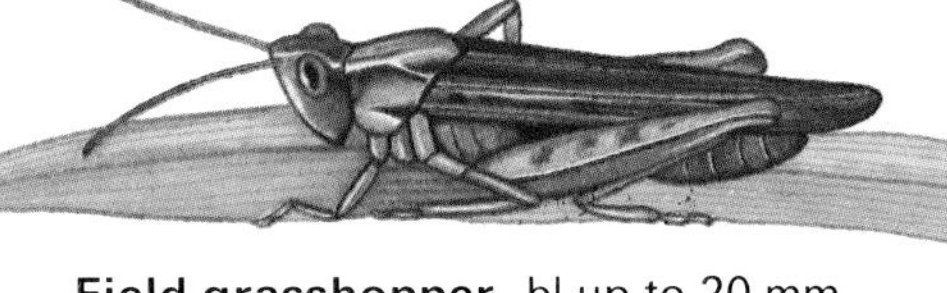

Field grasshopper bl up to 20 mm
Chorthippus brunneus. Very variable in colouring, though fully grown adults (in late summer) have noticeably long wings. Short chirping call. Worth learning calls of more common species, to make identification easier.

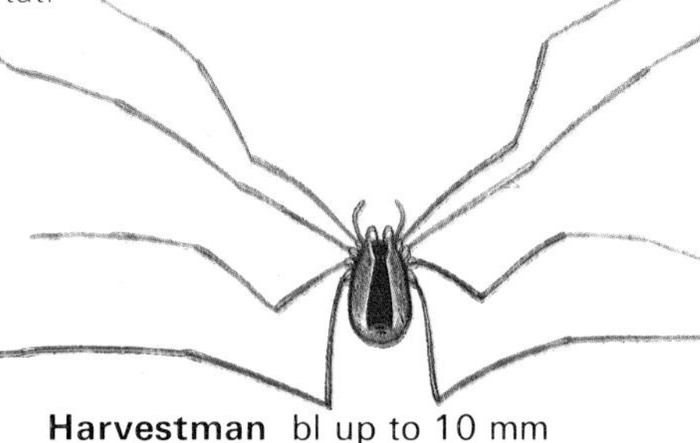

Harvestman bl up to 10 mm
Phalangium opilio. Looks rather like a spider, to which is closely related, but body is undivided, and usually has very long thin legs. Does not produce silk or venom, like a spider. Common everywhere in dense vegetation.

Large copper ws 34–40 mm
Lycaena dispar. Many species of copper butterflies exist. This is found in marshy fields throughout western Europe. Was extinct in Britain, but has recently been reintroduced. Easily recognized by fiery copper colour of wings. Larvae feed on dock leaves.

Spider
bl 12–15 mm (female), 10–12 mm (male)
Pisaura mirabilis. Attractive and distinctive spider, related to wolf spiders, which is often noticed because of its habit of making web tent over plant on which young spiderlings hatch. Female then sits on tent, acting as guardian.

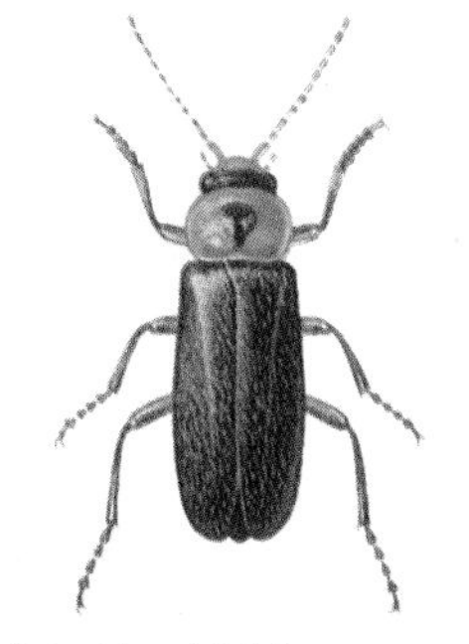

Soldier beetle bl 10 mm
Cantharis fusca. Fairly small beetle, with oblong shape and soft wing cases. Often found clinging to grass stems and flowers of meadow plants. Several different, but related beetles are given name 'soldier beetle'. Sometimes called 'bloodsucker' because of colour, but quite harmless. Visits flowers to catch other smaller insects.

Orange-tip butterfly
ws 33–48 mm
Anthocharis cardamines. This beautiful little butterfly is only one in northern or central Europe with orange tips to wings (though only male has this feature), so is quite distinctive. Flies in spring above damp meadows and around hedges.

BIRDS

Snipe bl 25 cm
Gallinago gallinago. Particular liking for damp meadows, where it breeds in early summer. Often conspicuous by male's strange 'drumming' flight – dives sharply and produces whirring noise from outer tail feathers.

Corn bunting bl 18 cm
Miliaria calandra. Rather undistinguished small brown bird, though readily recognizable in spring and summer by male's song. He perches on post or wire and produces noise like wheezing jangle of keys, unlike any other bird's song. Common in open country.

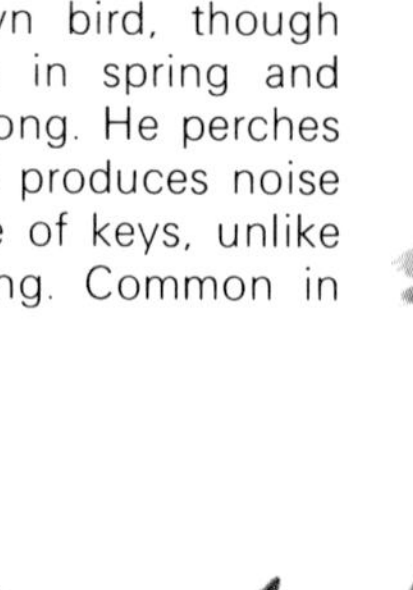

Yellowhammer bl 16.5 cm
Emberiza citrinella. Familiar hedgerow bird. Male's yellow head and chestnut-coloured rump is very conspicuous. Song, often likened to 'a little bit of bread and no cheese' – with last syllable drawn out – is particularly well-known.

Partridge bl 30 cm
Perdix perdix. Smallest of European partridges, and only one native to Britain, though rather similar red-legged partridge has been widely introduced. Common in open country over most of Europe, except far north.

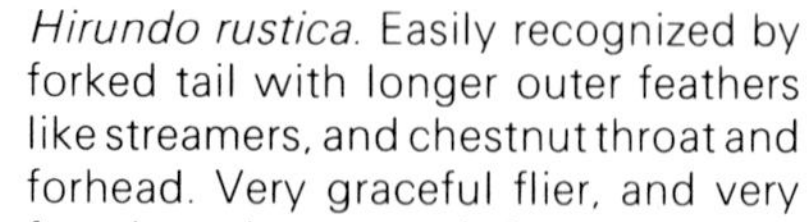

Swallow bl 18 cm
Hirundo rustica. Easily recognized by forked tail with longer outer feathers like streamers, and chestnut throat and forhead. Very graceful flier, and very fast, in order to catch insects on the wing. Sometimes seen flying close to surface of lakes and canals. Nests are made of mud, fixed to ledges of farm buildings. Migrates to Africa for winter months.

Redshank bl 27 cm
Tringa totanus. Beautiful wading bird. Spends much of year on coasts, but breeds mainly in damp tussocky pastures, especially where grazed by cattle. Long red legs are most conspicuous feature.

Pheasant bl 65–80 cm
Phasianus colchicus. Mainly ground-living bird, eating grain, seeds and berries. Has broad, round wings and long tail to allow maximum manoeuvrability. If startled, will fly up making noisy, whirring sound, but will not fly far. Breeds in open country with woods throughout western Europe.

Skylark bl 18 cm
Alauda arvensis. One of the most familiar birds of open country, with evocative song. Males sing for long periods, sometimes 5 minutes at a time, whilst hovering and circling around close to nest site, before finally plummeting to earth. Very common in open grassy places.

MAMMALS

Rabbit bl 34–45.5 cm
Oryctolagus cuniculus. Familiar everywhere throughout Europe, except in far north, though originally confined to parts of southern Europe, until introduced elsewhere. Although mainly nocturnal, can often be seen in the day if not regularly disturbed.

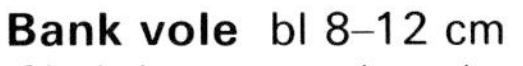

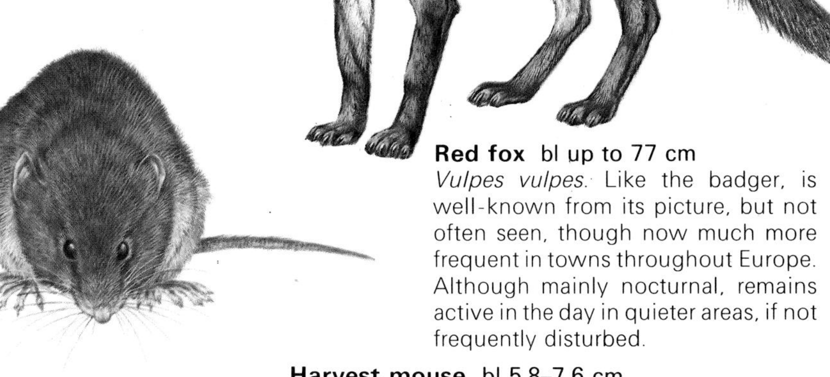

Bank vole bl 8–12 cm
Clethrionymus glareolus. Particularly common along hedgerows and banks, where there is both woody vegetation and grassy cover. Can climb surprisingly well in search of food, such as seeds and nuts, so is more often seen than other small mammals.

Red fox bl up to 77 cm
Vulpes vulpes. Like the badger, is well-known from its picture, but not often seen, though now much more frequent in towns throughout Europe. Although mainly nocturnal, remains active in the day in quieter areas, if not frequently disturbed.

Harvest mouse bl 5.8–7.6 cm
Micromys minutus. Tiny orangey-brown mouse, smallest of all European mice. Lives in all sorts of tall vegetation – not just in corn – and can most often be detected by presence of summer nest, which is ball of grass amongst stems.

Common shrew bl 7 cm
Sorex araneus. Unlike vegetarian mice and voles, shrews are highly carnivorous creatures, and need to find food almost all the time to maintain body heat and stay alive.

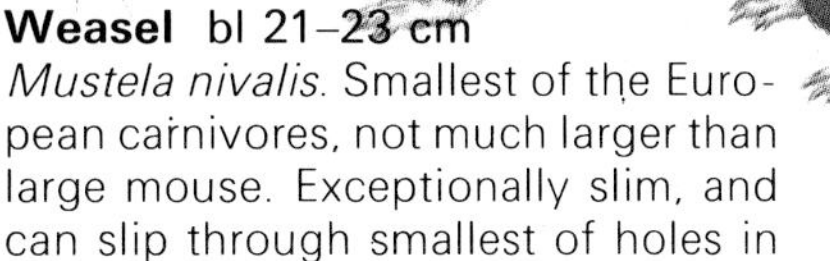

Weasel bl 21–23 cm
Mustela nivalis. Smallest of the European carnivores, not much larger than large mouse. Exceptionally slim, and can slip through smallest of holes in search of prey. Common throughout Europe in any rough grassy habitat.

Brown hare bl 48.5–67.5 cm
Lepus capensis. Rather like rabbit, and often confused with it, but hare has longer legs and ears, larger body, and ears have black tips. Much more solitary than rabbit, and usually prefers open country where it can escape from predators by running.

Mole bl 11.5–15 cm
Talpa europaea. Signs of its presence – molehills – are much more familiar than the animal itself. Strange, solitary creature that spends almost all of its life underground, just emerging occasionally, such as on wet nights, to feed on earthworms.

Stoat bl 22–29 cm
Mustela ermina. Very like a weasel, except for slightly larger size, and longer black-tipped tail. Agile and voracious predator, attacking birds and small mammals. Has been known to put on displays to attract inquisitive birds!

RIVERS, STREAMS AND PONDS

Freshwater habitats are a familiar feature of the European countryside. There can be few people who do not regularly visit ponds, lakes or rivers and water acts like a magnet to people as well as wildlife.

Some of our rivers, lakes and ponds are entirely natural, but many more are managed by man and some are completely man-made. Although man's influence does affect the *types* of plants and animals found in freshwater, every pond or stream will have plenty of interest in it.

PONDS AND LAKES

Unless man intervenes, ponds and lakes are not permanent features of the environment. Over the

Left: A common pondskater. These are very widely distributed throughout Britain and Europe. They use their front legs to grasp their prey, their middle legs as oars and their hind legs as rudders.

Below: A lowland river, flowing through lush water meadows, provides an important habitat for many plants, insects and birds.

years, they gradually accumulate more and more debris, and finally fill in completely. Silt is deposited from feed-streams and leaves fall in from the trees around the margins. As these decay, they form a thick sediment on the bottom and when this layer becomes deep enough, trees and shrubs take root. The appearance of trees is a sure sign that the pond or lake is near the end of its life. The final result is wet woodland such as alder carr.

To combat the natural process of in-filling, ponds and lakes are often cleaned of the bottom sediment and emergent vegetation, thus prolonging the life of the incumbent freshwater community.

If you visit a number of different ponds and lakes, you will soon notice that they harbour very different plants and animals. The type of freshwater community to be found depends on a number of different factors like the type of soil underlying the water, the size of the water body and whether it is found in lowland or upland areas.

In the hills and mountains of northern England and Scotland and northern Europe, the soils are very acid and this results in the water taking on this character. Very few insects can tolerate this extreme water chemistry and you are unlikely to find anything other than water beetles here. In lowland areas, however, the soils are often rich and sometimes contain chalk. Water in these regions contain lots of calcium which water snails use to make their shells.

Nowadays, much of the freshwater in lowland Britain and Europe is man-made. Reservoirs and gravel pits are a familiar sight. Although they lack the extensive community of plants and invertebrates found in natural lakes, they are often stocked with fish and attract large numbers of birds in the winter.

Gravel pits and reservoirs are a recent addition to freshwater habitats but even village ponds and farm ponds are generally man-made. Sited close to a human community they provided a ready supply of water for livestock before the advent of mains water and taps. In the Middle Ages, monks built stock ponds which held carp and tench – a living larder. Some of these ponds still exist, but at the start of the industrial revolution in the nineteenth century, many were turned into water supplies for early industry. Streams were also dammed and widened to make mill ponds, giving a guaranteed head of water to run flour mills.

POND AND LAKE LIFE

The amount of life below the surface of ponds and lakes is remarkable. Try pond-dipping and look at the amount of life in just one jar-full of water. The

Left: *Beautiful water crowfoot, flourishing in a river in France. It is generally found in slow-moving or stagnant water.*

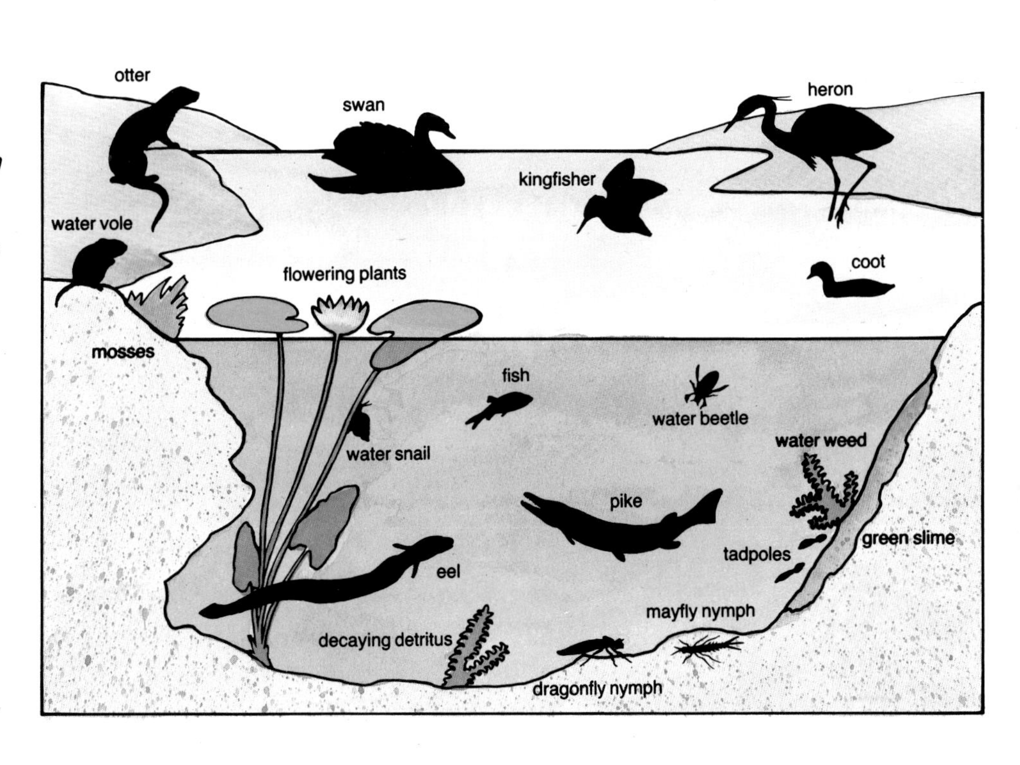

Right: *This diagram shows how some of the plants and animals in a lake interact with each other to their mutual benefit. The predators in the scheme help control numbers by culling the old, the diseased and the less well adapted.*

Pond-dipping

The only way to appreciate just what is going on in ponds is to have a close look, and collect some samples of the creatures that live there. It is amazing how much life there is, even in quite a small pond or stream.

Before doing anything else, take a little time to watch the water closely, and see what animals and plants you can see.

Once you have exhausted the possibilities of just watching, try a little dipping. Take a few trays (old ice-cream containers will do), some jars, and a sturdy pond net, such as those sold in aquarium shops. Don't bother with the cheap nets sold in holiday towns for rock-pool dipping – they are useless! After a few sweeps through the water, turn out your catch into the containers, and see what you have got. Individual creatures can be separated out, and examined in jars or small containers. Try rinsing strands of weed in water, to see what is hiding in them.

Larger pond animals will be immediately obvious in your pond sample. Dragonfly nymphs with their curious mask-like appendages, will shoot around the container, and water beetles scurry for cover. Smaller damselfly larvae crawl more sedately through the debris and are often well camouflaged and difficult to spot.

Some freshwater animals 'freeze' if disturbed, and you will be amazed what appears if you leave the container alone for a few minutes. The aptly named water stick-insect looks exactly like a twig until it moves and the fearsome water scorpion resembles a dead leaf.

Remember that many of the pond animals are very delicate and must be treated with care. Fish and tadpoles are also very sensitive and quickly die of lack of oxygen if not returned to the pond after a short period of observation. Make sure that you pour everything back. Don't forget the weeds and stones, and leave everything just as you found it.

A beautiful male great diving beetle, seen underwater amongst pond vegetation. This large beetle is common in ponds and stagnant waters and is to be found throughout the year.

pond is a whole self-contained habitat, with its own groups of predators, such as the dragonfly larvae or the voracious diving beetles and their extraordinary larvae; herbivores, such as the pond-snails and ramshorn snails, feeding on the plants; scavengers, such as the pond-skaters, and masses of decomposers feeding on the rotting material as it falls to the bottom. Some species spend their whole life in the water, while for quite a few others, it is just one phase of their existence.

Although some animals haunt the depths of the pond, others remain close to the surface. Pond skaters live up to their name and glide across the surface in search of animals trapped by the water. Water boatmen, on the other hand, search for food beneath the water's surface. They are sensitive to the least vibration and will congregate around a trapped moth. They have an advantage over pond skaters, however, because if danger threatens they can retreat to the pond's depths.

Many of the smaller pond creatures spend only part of their lives in water, emerging like dragonflies and mayflies to spend their adult life in the air. Amphibians, like frogs and toads, also only spend part of their life in water, retiring to the land during the winter months.

Fish, of course, have to spend their whole lives in water. In Britain nearly 40 species are to be found, from the tiny minnow to the giant-sized pike. Most fish tend to lay their eggs in the spring and shoals of spawning fish can often be seen in the shallow margins of the lake or pond. These congregations attract the attention of fish-eating birds like the kingfisher and heron. Ducks and moorhens feed on the submerged vegetation and often nest around the pond margin or in the dense cover of reeds and rushes.

RIVERS

Rivers are different from lakes or ponds because the eroding power of the constant flow of water, and occasional floods coming down the valley, prevents them from filling in.

We do not often get the chance to walk all the way down a river, from its source to the sea, partly because it is usually a very long way. If you do get the chance, especially along a shorter river with its source in some hills not far from the coast, it is a trip worth taking. Let us look at some of the changes that take place along the way.

RIVER LIFE

Most, though not all, rivers arise in the hills or mountains. In the highest stretches of the river, you will see that the water is fast-flowing and clear, frequently dropping over small falls. The base of the river is gravelly or rocky, with hardly any silt or mud, because any that does find its way into the water gets carried on down by the current. All this movement of the water makes it well-oxygenated, and of course it tends to be cold, especially if you are high in the mountains. Some plants and animals do well in this environment, while others are unable to survive at all. These higher reaches tend to be the zone of stone-flies and caddisflies, and the golden-ringed dragonfly; birds such as the dipper; and fishes that either live here permanently, such as the brown trout, or come up here to use the gravel as a spawning ground once a year, such as the salmon.

A little lower down, the river starts to slow down, and broaden out. Many more plants are now able to colonize, such as the water crowfoot, and there is more silt and mud in these slower stretches. The effect of having more plants is to create a more varied environment, and often this stretch of river is the richest in terms of its wildlife, unless it has become polluted by industry or agriculture. Fish life is abundant, with resident species, such as grayling or pike, and with various spawning species passing through.

Right: *This diagram shows some of the stages of a river on its way from the hills to the sea.*

Below: *An otter, an inhabitant of rivers and streams, eats a freshly-caught trout.*

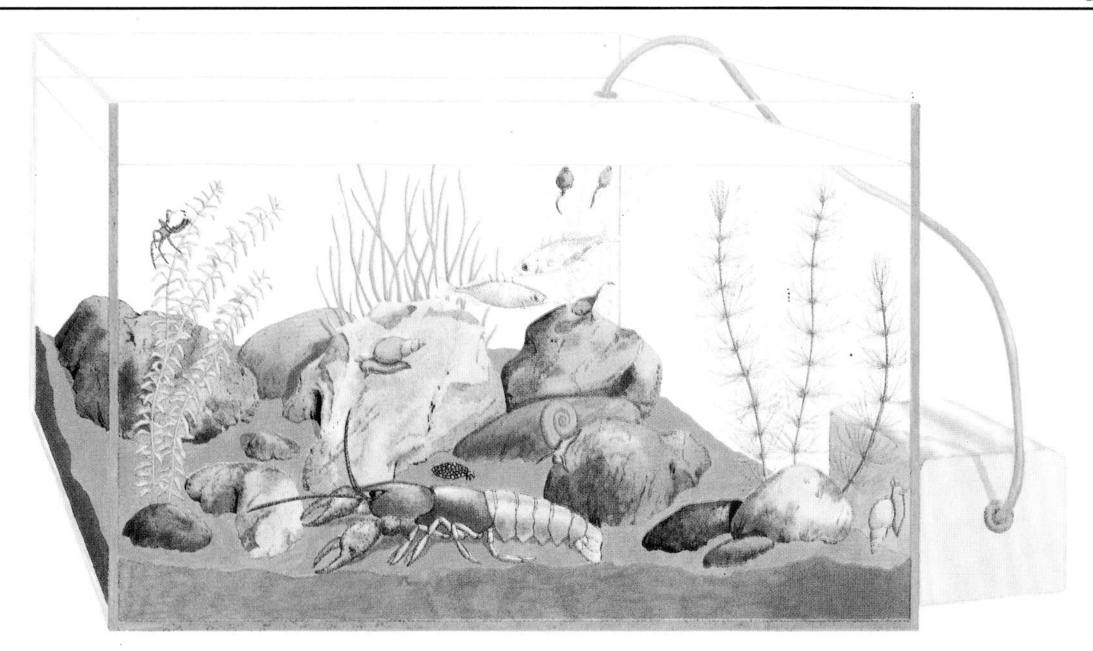

Setting up a home aquarium

The best way to study pond wildlife – and to photograph it – is to set up your own aquarium, and stock it with plants and animals from a nearby pond. First, put some clean sand or gravel, together with some stones, into a proper aquarium, not a curved fish bowl, glass is better than plastic, if you plan to do any photography. Then, fill the aquarium with clean water, preferably from a pond or rainwater butt. If you have to use tap-water, you should allow it to stand for a day to allow any anti-bacterial chemicals to evaporate.

The tank should be placed out of direct sunlight, but in a reasonable amount of light, and where you can easily see it. Stock it with a variety of plants, including some with floating leaves, and some that grow in the water, which will help to keep it oxygenated. Then, add the animal life (though some is bound to come with the plants anyway). Most small creatures will do well, as will some larger ones, such as sticklebacks. Do not put in large predators, such as diving beetle larvae, unless you have a large aquarium – they eat everything else! A few pond-dwellers fly, water boatmen for example, so don't be surprised if they appear in the room!

Once the aquarium becomes established, it should be virtually self-sustaining, but you can add extra things, such as tadpoles, or newts from time to time.

This can be an excellent area for the otter, that beautiful – but rare and declining – animal that depends on unpolluted and undisturbed rivers in which to fish. It is this section of river that is often selected as an otter haven, in other words a stretch of river where several neighbouring landowners have agreed to leave the banks undisturbed, to encourage otters back from the brink of extinction. Water-rats, voles and mink are also often to be found in and around their hides in the river's banks.

Birds too are plentiful on and around rivers. Ospreys, dippers, geese, ducks, kingfishers, herons and wagtails are amongst the most commonly found species. Lower down still, we reach the slow-flowing phase, where the course of the river meanders its way gently across flatter lands towards the sea. There is a lot of silt in the water, accumulated during the river's journey, and little is visible in the way of rocks or gravel. At times, the water has more the character of a lake or canal, and there may be dense areas of vegetation in the shallows. Sadly, this stretch rarely reaches its full potential in terms of wildlife. The pollution load, and the amount of agricultural fertilizer run-off, reach such high levels on most of the rivers of western Europe, that many species once common in such areas, such as the beautiful banded agrion damselfly, no longer occur.

Gradually, the river merges into the sea, depending on the slope of the land. In very low-lying flat coastal lands, the effects of the sea at high tide

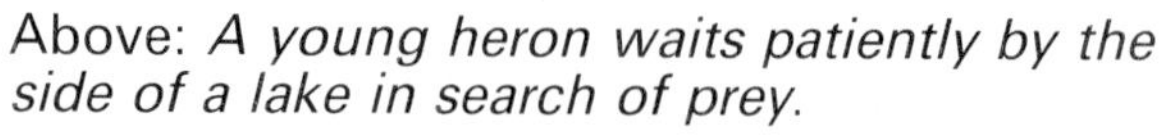

Above: *A young heron waits patiently by the side of a lake in search of prey.*

can reach many kilometres inland, while in other areas, the tidal effect is very small. This area, where freshwater and seawater meet, is known as the estuary, and it is one of the very richest environments of all for animals, with vast quantities of invertebrates surviving in its murky depths. Not surprisingly, these high densities of food attract many different kinds of birds, fishes, and marine mammals such as seals.

Left: *A male banded agrion damselfly perches on a riverside grass leaf.*

Below: *A large mayfly, seen here resting on grass, only lives for about a day. While closely resembling damselflies and dragonflies, these insects belong to a completely different order.*

Left: *The faceted eyes of a dragonfly are huge in proportion to body size when seen in close-up.*

Looking at dragonflies

Dragonflies are amongst the most exciting of insects to watch and study. They have even been called 'the birdwatcher's insect' because of their active behaviour and some of their odd habits. Many male dragonflies, for example, are territorial, and will defend a definite stretch of water against other males.

Dragonflies, and their close relatives the damselflies, breed in water; that is, they lay their eggs in or by water, and their young stages – the nymphs – develop in water, often taking many years. When they emerge as adults, they spend much of their time around water, feeding, mating, fighting or laying eggs, and you can observe most of these activities if you stop and watch. A pair of good close-focusing binoculars is a great asset for dragonfly-watching, incidentally. You may see brightly coloured males leaping from their perches to clash with other males, or grabbing duller-coloured passing females, to mate with. Sometimes they mate in mid-air, sometimes on the ground, and sometimes they even stay together while the female lays eggs into the water. Some of the damselflies even submerge themselves, climbing down plant stems to lay eggs.

Get up early on a midsummer morning, and you may be fortunate enough to see an exciting sight. Overnight, many dragonfly nymphs will have climbed out of the pond or stream, up some nearby vegetation; the process of changing into a winged dragonfly will have begun. This will take several hours, so watch and photograph it all at your leisure.

FLOWERS

Purple loosestrife ht 50–160 cm
Lythrum salicaria. One of the most attractive of waterside plants. Tall purple 'candles' of flowers are immediately visible from a distance. Flowers from July onwards, and has particular attraction for butterflies.

Ragged robin ht 30–70 cm
Lychnis flos-cuculi. Attractive and distinctive marshland and water's edge plant, with pink flowers with deeply slashed ragged petals. Occurs throughout western Europe, including mountain areas, flowering mainly in June.

Marsh marigold ht 15–50 cm
Caltha palustris. Common and familiar plant of marshes and pond edges. Flowers in spring, sometimes as early as March. Widespread throughout western Europe, even at high altitudes.

Flowering rush ht 50–150 cm
Butomus umbellatus. One of the more exotic-looking aquatic plants, with umbels of large pink lily-like flowers sticking up from water on tall stems. It occurs throughout western Europe in shallow water, though it is never very common.

Reedmace ht 90–250 cm
Typha latifolia. Reedmace, also often called bulrush (though there is another plant of that name) is abundant in and around edges of still waters throughout western Europe. Late in year, flower spikes break up into mass of fluffy seeds which disperse in wind.

Duckweed leaf dia 2-3 mm
Lemna minor. Smallest of European flowering plants. Leaves are only about 2–3 mm across, but flowers are even smaller, and rarely noticed. Floats on still, fresh waters, throughout western Europe, often carpeting entire surfaces with green leaves.

Frogbit ht 15–30 cm
Hydrocharis morsus-ranae. A true aquatic, with leaves floating on water surface looking like a miniature waterlily. Produces small white 3-petalled flowers in July and August, and is found in still waters throughout Europe.

White water-lily ht up to 2.5 m
Nymphaea alba. Most common and widespread of wild water-lilies, occurring on ponds and lakes throughout most of Europe. Begins to flower in June, then carries on through most of summer.

TREES AND SHRUBS

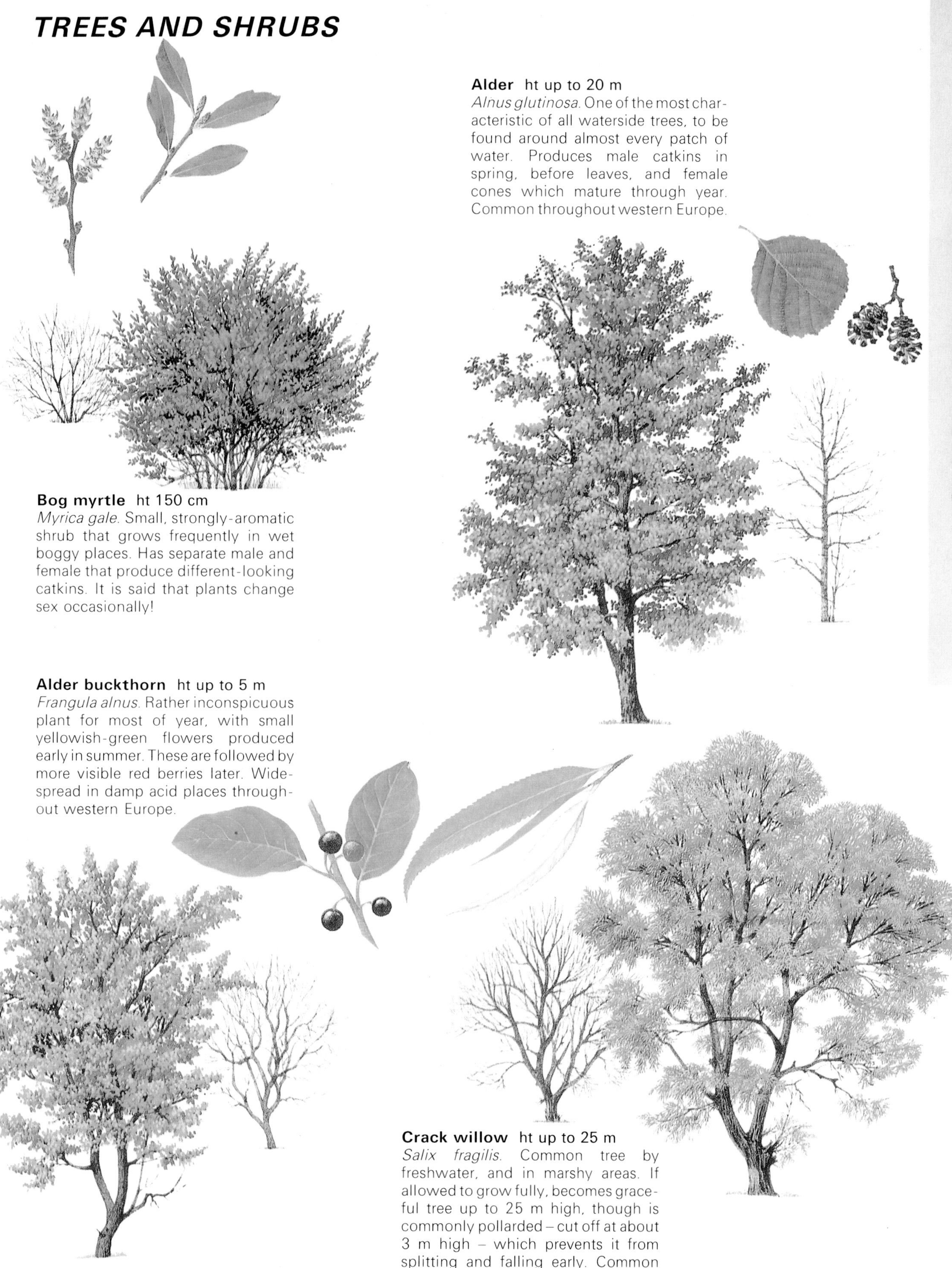

Alder ht up to 20 m
Alnus glutinosa. One of the most characteristic of all waterside trees, to be found around almost every patch of water. Produces male catkins in spring, before leaves, and female cones which mature through year. Common throughout western Europe.

Bog myrtle ht 150 cm
Myrica gale. Small, strongly-aromatic shrub that grows frequently in wet boggy places. Has separate male and female that produce different-looking catkins. It is said that plants change sex occasionally!

Alder buckthorn ht up to 5 m
Frangula alnus. Rather inconspicuous plant for most of year, with small yellowish-green flowers produced early in summer. These are followed by more visible red berries later. Widespread in damp acid places throughout western Europe.

Crack willow ht up to 25 m
Salix fragilis. Common tree by freshwater, and in marshy areas. If allowed to grow fully, becomes graceful tree up to 25 m high, though is commonly pollarded – cut off at about 3 m high – which prevents it from splitting and falling early. Common throughout western Europe.

INSECTS

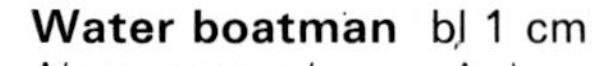

Water boatman bl 1 cm
Notonecta glauca. A bug that has taken almost entirely to aquatic life, and spends most of its time under water. Also called backswimmer because it swims upside-down, carrying large air bubble on its front.

Golden-ringed dragonfly
bl 54–61 mm (male), 61–65 mm (female)
Cordulegaster boltonii. Large and striking, one of few dragonflies to breed in running water. Most common on faster flowing acid streams. Females lay eggs by stabbing them into gravel at edge of stream.

Banded agrion bl 34–40 mm
Calopteryx splendens. Frequently seen around slow-flowing, rather calcareous, rivers. Blue spots on wings show up as flashing bands of colour when it flutters gently over water, looking almost like butterfly.

Swallowtail butterfly
ws 65–100 mm
Papilio machaon. Striking, beautiful and large. In some areas is dependent upon milk parsley, a marsh plant, for its larvae, so tends to be associated with wet places.

FISHES

Salmon bl 40–100 cm
Salmo salar. One of few fishes that people get a chance to see, because of habit of jumping up waterfalls and rapids when on way to spawning grounds. Spends part of life in rivers, but most is spent in sea.

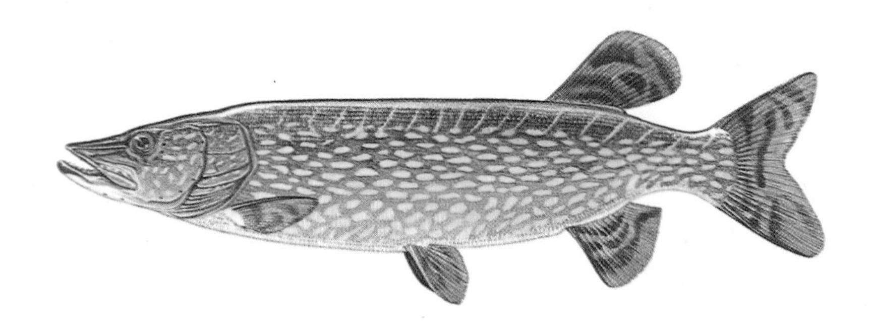

Pike bl 30–120 cm
Esox lucius. Large powerful predatory fish that lives in lakes and rivers, especially where there are weed beds in which it can hide. From here, darts out to catch passing fish. Common and widespread, though rarely seen.

Eel bl 40–90 cm
Anguilla anguilla. Familiar fish, looking more like water-snake than fish. Common in freshwater everywhere, though returns to sea to breed, in an extraordinary journey. Able to cross land areas, especially on wet nights, should need arise.

Three-spined stickleback
bl 4–8 cm
Gasterosteus aculeatus. Small, but familiar fish, often seen in ponds and rivers. Has 2 or 3 long spines on its back. In early summer, male becomes more highly coloured, and builds nest for female to lay eggs into.

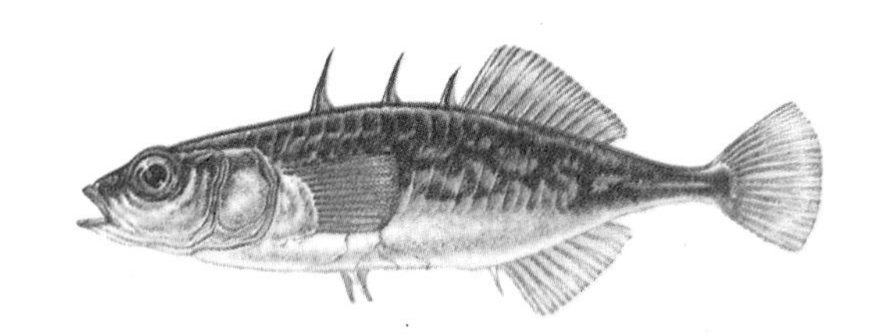

AMPHIBIANS

Common toad bl 8–12 cm
Bufo bufo. Common over most of Europe, wherever there is suitable habitat. Breeds in large ponds, and tends to come back to the same pond every year, often in very large numbers. Spawn is laid in strings, unlike the masses of frog-spawn.

Common frog
bl 9 cm (female), 7 cm (male)
Rana temporaria. Probably most widespread amphibian in western Europe. Breeds in all waters, including very acid pools, and even tiny puddles, and can be found at considerable heights on mountains. Masses of jelly-like spawn are familiar sight in spring.

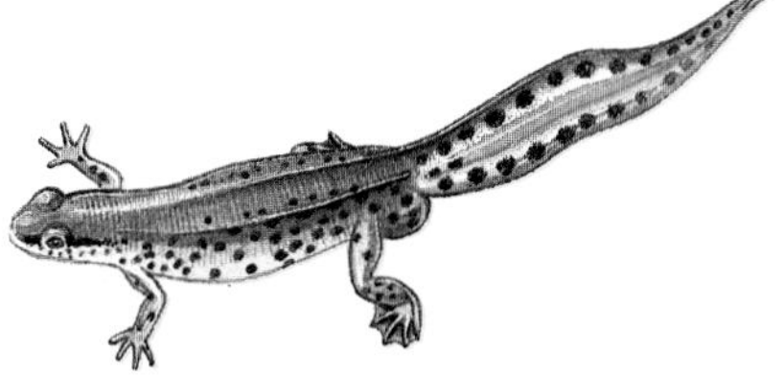

Smooth newt bl 8–9 cm
Triturus vulgaris. Often called common newt as is probably most common and widespread of newts. Comes to ponds in spring to breed. For rest of year is found in drier habitats, though rarely far from water.

Palmate newt bl 8–9 cm
Triturus helveticus. Smallest of European newts. Often hard to distinguish female from smooth newt, but male easily recognized, particularly in breeding season, by thread-like filament at end of tail and swollen webs of hind feet.

BIRDS

Tufted duck bl 43 cm
Aythya fuligula. Second in familiarity and tolerance of man only to mallard. Tufted ducks are distinctively coloured, and males, in particular, have characteristic drooping tuft of feathers at the back. Common through north and central Europe.

Great-crested grebe bl 48 cm
Podiceps cristatus. One of the most distinctive of water birds, and largest European grebe. In breeding season, adults have black crest, and broad frills on sides of face, though these disappear in winter. Widespread, except in far north.

Grey wagtail bl 18 cm
Motacilla cinerea. Jaunty and attractive little bird, resident on rivers and streams throughout central Europe. Exists happily close to buildings, though it also occurs in some of the most remote areas in hills.

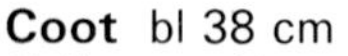

Coot bl 38 cm
Fulica atra. Very common and familiar water bird, breeding on open still waters throughout western Europe. Unlike some of the rail family, is aggressive and fearless, even learning to take food from humans at times. Normal food consists of water plants, reached by diving.

Sedge warbler bl 12.5 cm
Acrocephalus schoenobaenus. Easily recognized by striped head, buff eyestrip and square-ended tail. Breeds in coarse vegetation, bushes and hedges near water throughout most of Europe.

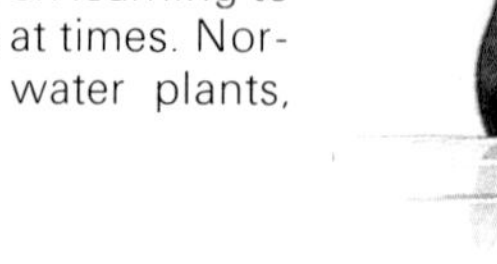

Mallard bl 58 cm
Anas platyrhynchos. Probably most common and familiar duck over most of Europe. Occurs wild in most wetland areas, and is also introduced widely into farmyard ponds and ornamental lakes. Call is typical 'quacking' expected from ducks.

Kingfisher bl 16.5 cm
Alcedo atthis. One of the most dashing and familiar of water birds, though few people have actually had good clear view of one. Surprisingly small, but makes up for it by brilliant colouring. Widespread, except in north.

Grey heron bl 90 cm
Ardea cinerea. Familiar sight, standing motionless in shallows of a lake or river, or flying overhead with distinctive slow flight and hunched neck. Common and widespread over most of Europe, except far north of Mediterranean.

MAMMALS

Coypu bl 60 cm
Myocastor coypus. Large semi-aquatic rodent, almost as large as a beaver, though lacking flattened tail. Introduced from North America, but well-established in eastern England and France in marshy areas with open water and ditches.

Otter bl 80 cm
Lutra lutra. One of most beautiful and graceful mammals in Europe. Highly adapted to life in water, and can swim above or below surface with great speed, either when playing, or in search of prey. Has declined considerably, especially in highly-farmed areas.

Water shrew bl 9 cm
Neomys fodiens. Most shrews tend to live in damp places, where their food is easily found, but water shrews are particularly associated with water, and will often take to it in search of prey. Like common shrew, must eat constantly. Actually eat roughly their own body weight every day.

Daubenton's bat bl 5 cm ws 27 cm
Myotis daubentoni. Usually roosts and breeds in houses and caves, but are particularly adapted for feeding over water. Can fly very close to surface, using shallow wing beats, to pick off emerging insects. Widespread, but not common.

Mink bl 40 cm
Mustela vison. Most widespread species in western Europe is North American mink, which has escaped from fur farms. There is also native European species in eastern Europe. Voracious predator, able to take to water as necessary, though also at home on land.

Water vole bl 19 cm
Arvicola terrestris. Much larger than most voles, reaching roughly size of a rat, though has much shorter tail. Usually seen near water, and can swim well and dive, though spends much time out of water.

THE SEASHORE

The seashore is an extraordinary and exciting habitat where we can glimpse exotic animals from the marine world. For many of us, the most familiar type of seashore is the sandy beach where we spend our holiday. However, there are many other types of shore, including rocky shores, cliffs, shingle beaches and mudflats.

As you probably know, the seas around our coasts rise and fall twice a day, and these movements are known as tides. However, the extent of the tidal range varies around the shores. In some areas there is a difference between high and low tide of only a couple of metres, whereas in the mouth of the Bristol Channel for example, the tidal range is nearly 12 metres. The animals and plants on the shore experience different

The incredible sight of a gannet colony on an offshore island in early summer.

A coastal lagoon in southern France is rich in bird and invertebrate life.

periods of submersion in seawater and exposure to air. Because each species has its own preferences, they occur in well-defined areas of the shore and the resulting 'zonation' holds true from one part of a country to another.

Zonation is most easily seen on a rocky shore. Above the high tide line, orange lichens mark the splash zone and below this the zones are given the names of the most frequent seaweed species that occurs there.

SOME TYPES OF COAST

Take a look at some of the varied types of coast and why they occur.

Cliffs can be found wherever hills meet the sea. If the rock is very soft, the cliffs are rarely steep, while harder rocks form sheerer cliffs. Chalk, however, although not especially hard, forms dramatic sheer cliffs which are undercut and later collapse. Cliffs can be wonderful places for wildlife depending on the type of rock. Sometimes it forms ledges which support vast colonies of seabirds. Razorbills, guillemots, puffins, fulmars, kittiwakes and gulls all compete for nesting space. If the rock erodes enough to form a little soil, flowers such as sea campion, thrift and wild cabbage find footholds in the crevices.

Shingle beaches are very impressive, though not too popular with holidaymakers, as they are difficult to walk on. They are made up of millions of rounded stones, from the size of peas up to the size of potatoes, or even larger. They are usually formed where a current drifts across an estuary or bay, and deposits its larger stones after each storm, and they often form into hook-shaped promontories or long bars. At first, very little can grow on them, but as they stabilize, plants like yellow horned poppy, sea-pea and sea-kale come in. If the shingle is not washed away again, it eventually becomes grass-covered, and trees or heathland will eventually take its place. The shores off shingle beaches support very little marine life because of the abrasive stones. However, above the tideline, nesting gulls and terns form large colonies.

Rocky shores. For the naturalist, the rocky shores around our coasts are the richest habitats to search. Below the tideline, seaweeds festoon the rocks. Because they are pounded by waves, they have strong holdfasts which attach them to the rocks. Crabs and small fish find shelter amongst these holdfasts and venture out when calm conditions prevail.

Some rocky shores are exposed to the full force of the elements. Barnacles, limpets and encrusting seaweeds are among the few things which can survive these harsh conditions. In more settled spots, anemones and starfish are common and easily found.

Rockpools are depressions in the rock which

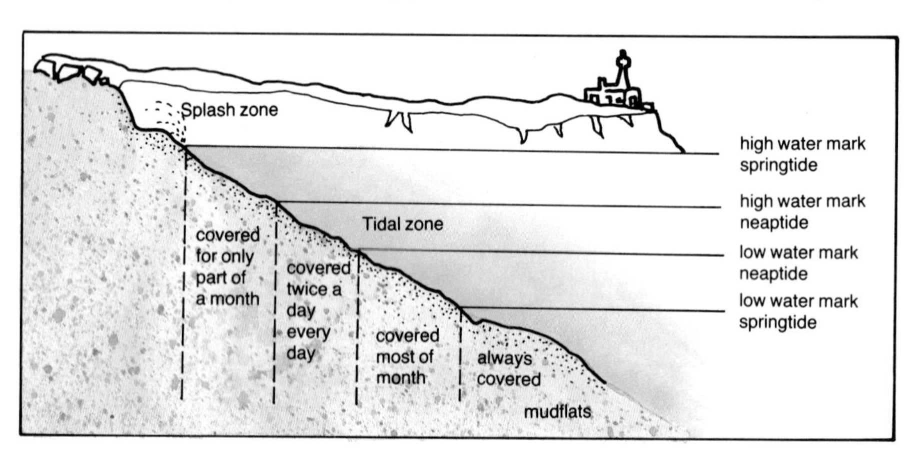

Left: *A diagram showing how different tide levels cover different parts of a beach. The tides are the results of the pulls of gravity of the sun and the moon.*

Right: *A shingle beach in southern England. The heights of the recent tides are clearly marked by the strand lines. The eroded chalk slopes beyond testify to the cutting power of the sea.*

Below: *A close view of the rounded pebbles, mostly flints and quartz, on a shingle beach, caused by the buffeting of waves and sea currents.*

fill with seawater as the tide goes out. If they are high up the shore, they are open to the elements for much of the day, and may get warmed by the sun, or diluted by rain; lower down the shore, they are cushioned from these effects by being submerged under the sea for longer.

Rockpool animals have to be tolerant of a harsh and changeable environment. The best time of year to look for them is at the lowest tides when the lowest pools are exposed. The lowest tides are called spring tides but occur once a month. Most seaside towns give information about the dates and times of day when they occur.

If possible, start your investigation when the tide is high, and work down the shore as the tide retreats. This means that you can look at each rockpool in turn, as it becomes exposed, and work out the pattern down the shore. It is also the safest way to explore the shore because you are less likely to be trapped by the tide.

You may not be able to identify everything you find, even with the help of a good guide, but you will quickly spot new species, such as a different sort of sea anemone when it appears. Right at the lowest tide level, you may start to find some exciting things, not at all like those further up. These may be truly marine creatures accidentally trapped in the pool. Keep notes on what you find, and try to work out any patterns of distribution.

Sandy beaches occur where the sea currents subside and allow the sand to settle. Often this takes place in little bays between rocky headlands,

out of the full force of the waves or sometimes in long strands, if the current movement is right. At first glance, sandy beaches may appear uninteresting and devoid of life. They are, however, rich in wildlife if you know how and where to look. To escape the force of the waves, most of the animals such as sea urchins, lugworms, ragworms and bivalve molluscs, bury themselves. By looking for the tell-tale signs of displaced sand and so on, you can easily locate their burrows.

Sometimes sandy beaches are backed by a line of sand-dunes that are hills of sand, blown inland from the beach. These gradually become colonized by plants, unless they are constantly blown away. Most species are specially adapted to the dry, hot, salty and unstable conditions. Sea-holly,

A common seal pup, on a muddy beach. Numbers of these delightful creatures have been decimated by a killer virus which has been sweeping coastal waters.

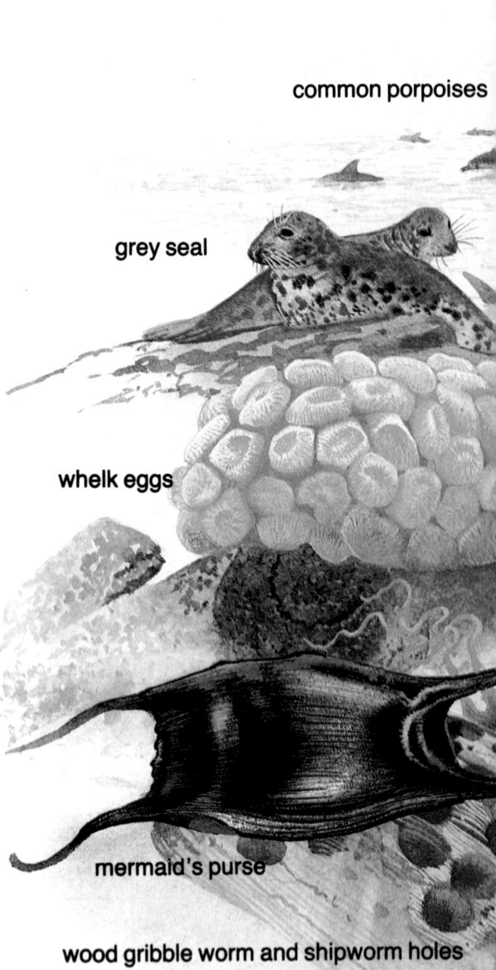

PROJECT

Beach-combing

'Beach-combing', or, in other words, searching beaches for anything that has been washed up, is fascinating – you never know what will turn up. If possible, go to the beach just after high tide, and so much the better if there was a storm the night before, as more will be washed up.

What you find will be an interesting blend of natural and man-made objects, and – depending on the currents around your particular beach – they may come from many parts of the world. For example, you may find the 'mermaid's purses' that are really dogfish egg-cases, or the 'cuttle-bone' which is the internal skeleton of the strange cuttlefish. Shells of all kinds may abound, including unfamiliar and possibly tropical ones. However, you will also find driftwood, in all different shapes and sizes; tins, bottles (look out for messages!), and all sorts of other man-made debris.

A few words of warning. Avoid any unopened cans that might contain chemicals, and report their presence to the coastguard. And wear old clothes. So many beaches today have oil washed up on them, that you are always likely to get some on you.

Have fun.

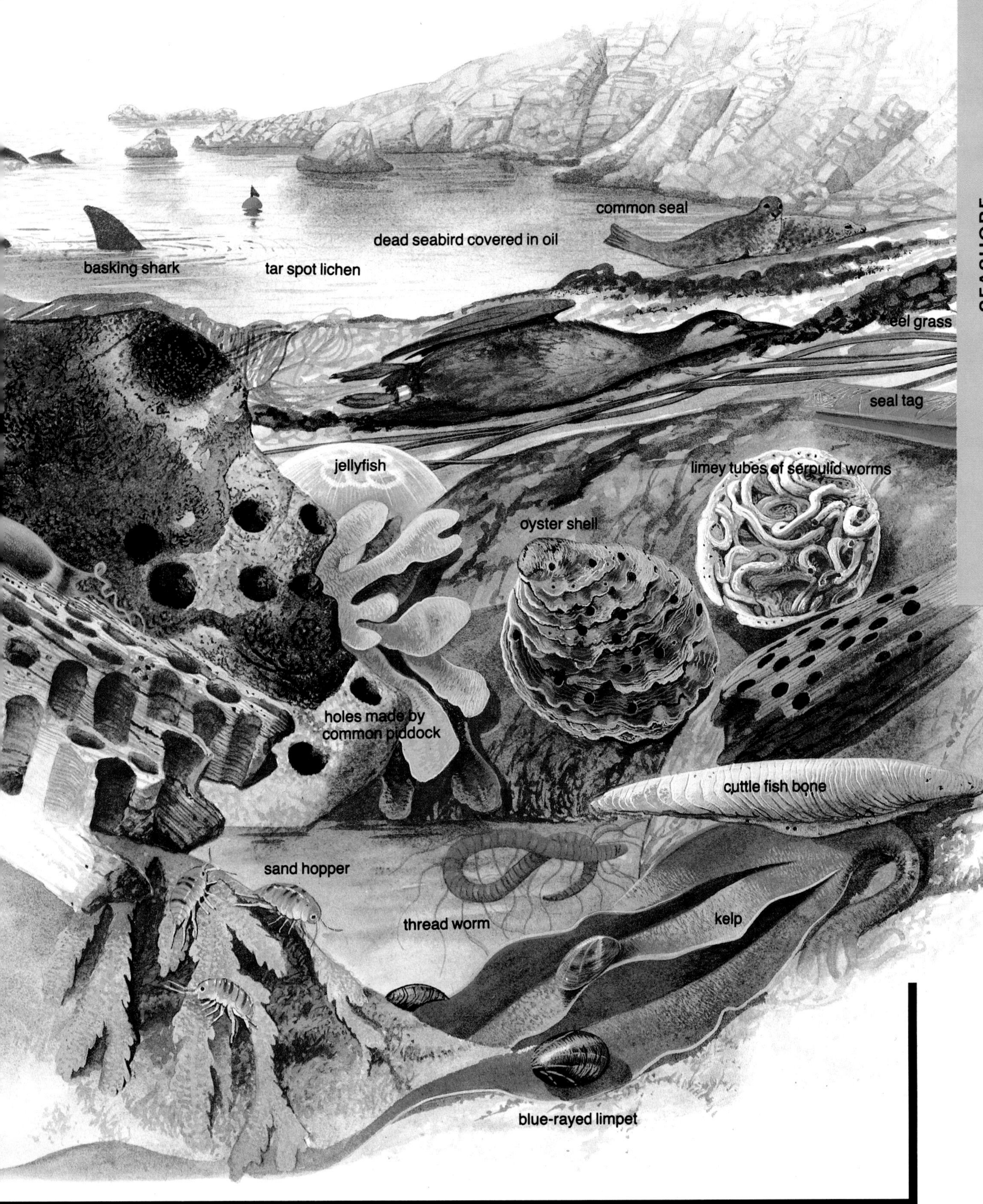
common seal
dead seabird covered in oil
basking shark
tar spot lichen
eel grass
seal tag
jellyfish
limey tubes of serpulid worms
oyster shell
holes made by common piddock
cuttle fish bone
sand hopper
thread worm
kelp
blue-rayed limpet

Left: *Marram grass, with its extensive rooting system, has helped to form this sand dune.*

Below: *A section across a dune system, (the sea on the left), shows how the dunes gradually become stable.*

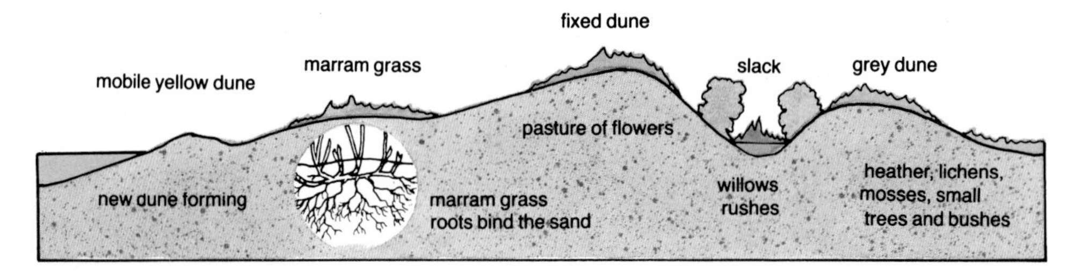

sea-bindweed and marram grass are common and terns of various kinds commonly nest in stable sand-dunes, except where disturbed by holidaymakers.

The dunes tend to keep on forming and moving inland, so stable dunes with vegetation are found furthest away from the sea, and younger, whiter dunes next to the beach.

Mudflats and saltmarshes occur in sheltered places such as estuaries and bays. Mud is the very finest of silt, so it is only deposited where the currents are very weak. At low tide, estuaries become a glistening mass of mudflats, which are wonderful places for birds, especially in winter. Although mudflats may appear inhospitable, they support countless millions of molluscs and crustaceans buried beneath the surface. Huge numbers of waders, ducks and geese congregate on the mudflats to feed on these invertebrates, or the green algae and eel-grass that also grows there.

Where the water is shallow and gently-sloping, saltmarsh plants become established. These are mainly flowering plants that are able to tolerate seawater, and can even stand total immersion for a short while. Sea-lavender, sea purslane and saltmarsh grasses are the most conspicuous species found. Gradually, the upper layers of the saltmarsh raise themselves above regular high-tide level, and start to get away from the effects of the sea. These upper saltmarshes are good places for birds such as redshank to breed, though their eggs are occasionally washed out by a high tide.

Right: *A beautiful snakelocks anemone, with its waving mass of tentacles, in a rock pool.*

Below: *A mixed flock of waders, mainly knots, godwits and oystercatchers, wintering on mudflats and estuaries.*

Looking at seaweeds

Seaweeds are simple, primitive plants, part of the group of plants known as algae, that do not produce flowers. They are adapted for life around the tideline, particularly on rocky shores, where they can gain a stronger foothold.

If you can find a gently shelving, rocky shore, you will notice that the seaweeds appear in definite bands along the shore, not grouped just by different species, but in different colours, too. The green seaweeds tend to be in a band near the top of the shore, whilst various sorts of brown seaweeds occupy the middle of the inter-tidal zone, with the redder seaweeds at the bottom, extending below the low-water mark. It is not always so well defined, but these bands can often be clearly seen.

There are two reasons for this; first, different species can stand varying amounts of time out of seawater. The ones at the top of the shore can survive the most exposure and may only be covered for an hour or so at high tide,and the rest of the time they may be baked by the sun, or inundated by rain, while those at the low-water mark are more delicate and need to be submerged most of the time. Secondly, the seaweeds have developed a range of pigments to deal with the different sorts of light that reach the various depths of water. The green upper-shore ones get most normal light, so they are most like ordinary green plants; further down the shore, they depend more and more on the blue light that filters through the sea, so they are a different colour to help absorb it.

Above: *A giant kelp, covered with other seaweed, growing on the lowest tide level.*

Below: *A huge clump of knotted wrack growing in a sheltered bay.*

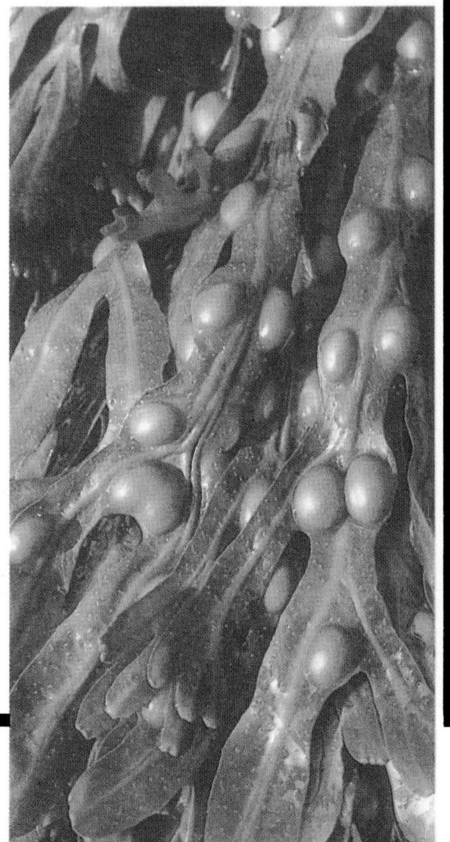

Below: *The familiar bladder-wrack, with its popping air bladders, grows in the middle of a rocky shore.*

Feeding the crabs

There are plenty of crabs everywhere, especially on certain mixed sandy and stony beaches, but they are timid creatures that prefer hiding to coming out and biting you! If you spot one going under a stone, or suspect that one is there, you can try tempting it out with a morsel of food. Meat is their favourite, though other foods may do the trick. If the crab is submerged, try dangling the food on a line just by the hole – and maybe haul in the string if it does bite, so that you get a closer view. When the tide is out, try putting the food out on the beach by the hole, and then wait quietly to see if you are lucky.

A shore crab amongst sea lettuce.

PROJECT

Watching shellfish feeding

Most shell-fish, such as limpets, periwinkles, and barnacles, stop feeding when the tide is out, and so they are rarely seen. You can observe some of this behaviour quite simply though, without having to create a seawater aquarium. Find a small stone with some barnacles on it – they are common on many beaches – and put it into an old ice-cream container with some seawater in it. A glass jar will do if the stone is small enough. After a while, the barnacles will open up the tops of their shells, and start to wave their little 'tentacles' about in search of food. When you have finished, take the barnacles out of the water and watch them closely. Remember to put them back exactly where you found them.

Barnacles feeding underwater, with their tentacles extended.

SEAWEEDS

Toothed wrack l c 60 cm
Fucus serratus. Distinguishable from other wracks by its toothed fronds, which may grow to about 60 cm long. Occurs on lower inter-tidal areas, often in a distinctive band. Common on rocky shores throughout western Europe.

Bladderwrack l 15–100 cm
Fucus vesiculosus. Probably the best-known of the brown seaweeds, because of soft bladders, that 'pop' as you walk over them. Abundant around all rocky coasts, forming distinctive band in middle shore zone.

Laver l 5–20 cm
Porphyra umbilicalis. Strange species, with gelatinous purplish fronds coming from one base. Variable in shape, but usually distinctive. Edible and often collected. Common throughout on rocky shores, especially where sandy.

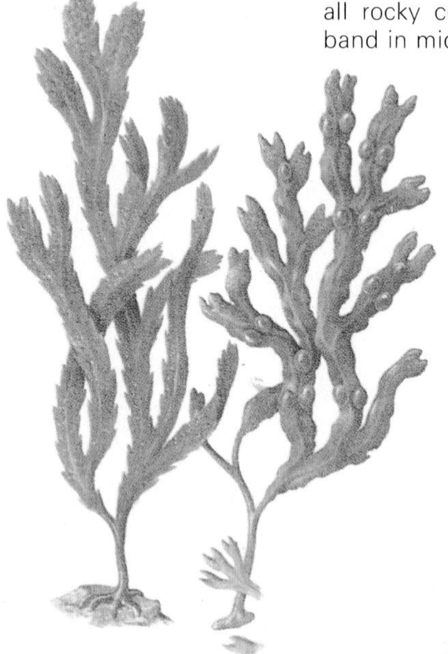

Oar weed l c 1m
Laminaria digitata. Distinctive seaweed, with divided frond on thick stalk. Usually grows below low-water mark, but often washed up, when it turns green, then white. Rocky coasts throughout western Europe.

Dulse 10–30 cm
Palmaria palmata. Expands from original disc-like shape to form a flattened 'fan'. Occurs on rocks on middle and lower shores and in shallow waters.

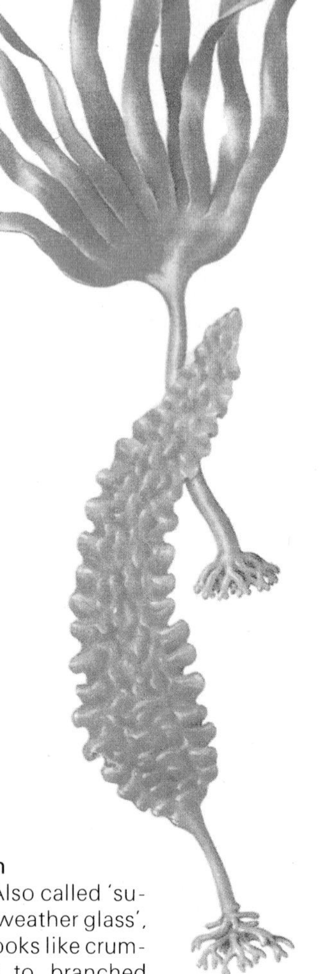

Channelled wrack l 5–15 cm
Pelvetia canaliculata. Very abundant seaweed that occurs all round coasts, usually in upper parts of shore, and even above high-tide level if spray reaches it. Fronds short, up to 15 cm long.

Sea lettuce l 15–100 cm
Ulva lactuca. Aptly-named for its broad soft green fronds. Occurs commonly in many situations, both inter-tidal and submerged, and on all coast types throughout western Europe except most exposed.

Sea belt l 20 cm–3 m
Laminaria saccharina. Also called 'sugar belt' or 'poor man's weather glass', because of past uses. Looks like crumpled ribbon, attached to branched holdfast, on rocks and stones. Common throughout on suitable coasts.

FLOWERS

Yellow horned poppy
ht up to 75 cm
Glaucium flavum. Frequent plant of sandy and shingly coasts throughout western Europe. After producing beautiful golden yellow flowers, from midsummer onwards, produces very long curved pods, up to 30 cm.

Thrift ht 20–40 cm
Armeria maritima. Very common and distinctive coastal plant, on rocky cliffs, grassy areas, and even mud. Also occasionally inland, especially in mountains. Flowers from April through summer. Widespread throughout.

Sea aster ht up to 90 cm
Aster tripduim. Pink flowered, this plant towers over other coast and marshland plants. Occasionally seen inland.

Sea lavender ht up to 30 cm
Limonium vulgare. Flat-topped heads of purple flowers, it is abundant in middle marshland and coasts.

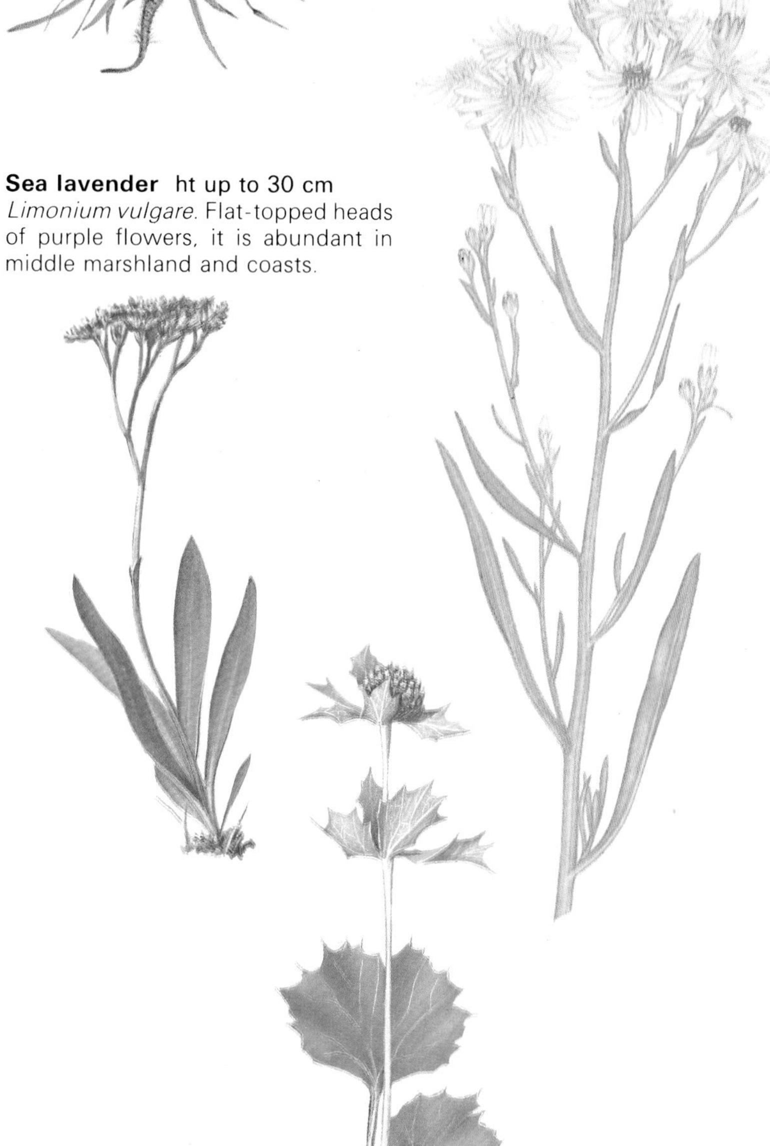

Sea campion ht up to 25 cm
Silene maritima. Abundant plant on rocky cliffs and shingle, flowering in masses in cushions from April onwards. Common throughout coastal areas, occasionally also on mountains.

Sea holly ht 10–40 cm
Eryngium maritimum. Distinctive electric-blue spiny plant, occurring commonly on dunes and shingle all around coasts, never inland. Flowers in June–September.

INVERTEBRATES

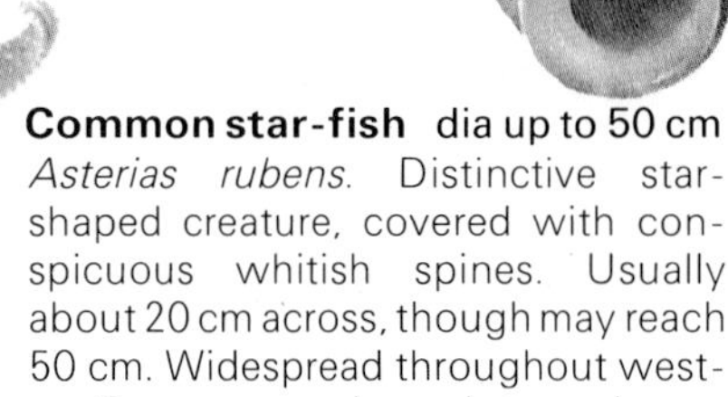

Periwinkle ht c 2.5 cm
Littorina littorea. Common and widespread seashell, that occurs on rocks and seaweeds around coasts of north-west Europe. Concentric rings of darker lines help to distinguish it from similar species.

Common star-fish dia up to 50 cm
Asterias rubens. Distinctive star-shaped creature, covered with conspicuous whitish spines. Usually about 20 cm across, though may reach 50 cm. Widespread throughout western Europe on rocky and stony shores.

Common mussel bl 1–10 cm
Mytilus edulis. Common and well-known edible mussel, sold in shops. Occurs in vast beds on sandy and muddy shores. Widespread throughout the area.

Beadlet anemone ht up to 7 cm
Actinia equina. One of commonest and most familiar rock pool creatures, occurring on rocky coasts all over north-west Europe. Colour varies from brown to red. Also a 'strawberry form' with yellow dots.

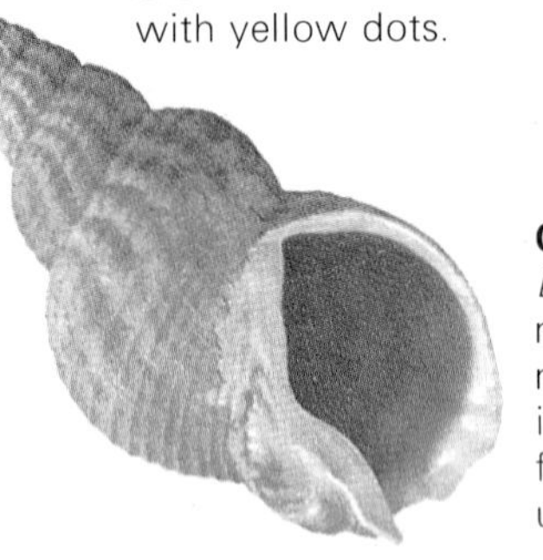

Common whelk ht up to 8 cm
Buccinum undatum. Large shell common and widespread on sandy and muddy shores. When empty, often inhabited by hermit crabs. Strange frothy egg-masses are often washed up on the shore.

Common shore crab bl up to 4 cm
Carcinus maenas. Probably most familiar crab, occurring commonly on sandy and muddy beaches throughout western Europe. Up to 5 cm across, usually less, and green or greyish in colour.

FISHES

Montagu's blenny bl up to 8 cm
Blennius montagui. Small, but rather distinctive fish that occurs in rock pools and shallow rocky water around the coasts from south-west Britain southwards.

Sea trout bl up to 1 m
Salmo trutta. Close relative of salmon, with similar habits. Occurs in coastal waters throughout western Europe for most of year, moving up rivers to spawn. Common.

Flounder bl up to 20 cm
Platichthys flesus. Typical small flatfish that lives flat in mud or sand of shallow offshore waters. Can also tolerate less salty waters, and occurs well up in estuaries.

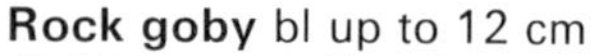

Lesser spotted dogfish bl up to 1 m
Sciliorhynus canicula. Medium-sized relative of sharks. Common around coasts in shallow water with sand or gravel bottom.

Rock goby bl up to 12 cm
Gobius paganellus. Common inhabitant of rock pools, especially lower down the beach, throughout western coastal areas, as far north as Scotland. Often caught by people investigating rock pools.

Greater black-backed gull bl 64–69 cm
Larus marinus. Very large and powerful gull, with noticeably black back. Spends more time at sea than most, but breeds on coast, often amongst other seabirds, which it preys on.

Gannet bl 90 cm
Sula bassana. Attractive and unmistakable bird when seen at close quarters. Breeds in large colonies, often on islands, in an area centred around Britain, though birds travel widely for rest of year.

Ringed plover bl 19 cm
Charadrius hiaticula. Attractive and gregarious little wader, with conspicuously coloured plumage, and melodic call. Breeds commonly on sandy and muddy coasts throughout northern Europe.

Shag bl 76 cm
Phalacrocorax aristotelis. Smaller and slimmer version of cormorant, with less white. Common throughout coasts of north-west Europe, and much less likely to be seen inland than cormorant.

Sanderling bl 20 cm
Calidris alba. Whitest of European waders, so easily picked out on the ground or in flight. Winters on sandy, or occasionally rocky European coasts, and breeds in high arctic.

Eider bl 58 cm
Somateria mollissima. Largest European duck, and one of the most distinctive, with long sloping head profile and distinctive colouring. Spends virtually all its life in and around sea off north European coasts.

Herring gull bl 56 cm
Larus argentatus. Familiar sight in coastal areas, and increasingly inland. Large aggressive gull common everywhere around coasts, and frequently a problem where other, rarer, birds are nesting.

Cormorant bl 90 cm
Phalacrocorax carbo. Largest of the European cormorants, distinguishable from shags by greater bulk, and by noticeable white cheeks and throat. Breeds around the coasts of northern Europe, less frequently inland.

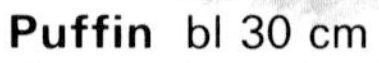

Puffin bl 30 cm
Fratercula arctica. One of most familiar and comical of birds, from its pictures, though few people have actually seen one. Breeds in colonies on rocky coasts in northern Europe, becoming more marine for rest of the year.

Wigeon bl 46 cm
Anas penelope. This duck breeds in tundra and open moorland areas through northern Europe. In winter gathers in large flocks on estuaries and coastal marshes, throughout Europe.

Knot bl 25 cm
Calidris canuta. Inconspicuous wader, most often seen in huge flocks on coasts in winter. Breeds in arctic, but winters round many European shores, especially at estuaries.

Turnstone bl 23 cm
Arenaria interpres. Attractive and confiding little wader, with lovely marbled plumage. Spends its time scavenging along shore, turning over stones, seaweed, and anything else, in search of food. Common and widespread.

Oystercatcher bl 43 cm
Haematopus ostralegus. One of the most distinctive of coastal birds, with its bright colour scheme and loud persistent whistling call, especially in breeding season. Common on coast, occasionally inland.

MAMMALS

Grey seal bl up to 3.2 m
Halichoerus grypus. Occurs over a wider area than the common seal, and tends to favour rockier, more exposed coasts. Its straight 'Roman' nose profile is a useful identification aid.

Common seal bl up to 1.9 m
Phoca vitulina. Widespread and moderately common throughout the coasts of northern Europe, usually occurring in sheltered areas where there are sandbanks. Quite sociable, though not as noisy and gregarious as grey seals.

Common porpoise bl up to 1.8 m
Phocoena phocoena. Smallest member of porpoise family, up to about 1·8 m long. Widespread throughout European seas, often in small groups. Does not jump out of the water like dolphin, and is generally less active.

Dolphin bl up to 2.4 m
Delphinus delphis. Slightly larger than the porpoise, but noticeably more active, often diving and leaping in 'schools' alongside ships. Widespread throughout Europe, except further north.

Pilot whale bl up to 8.6 m
Globicephala melaena. Seen quite regularly, especially off northern and western coasts of Britain. Usually occurs in small schools, which used to be cut off by local fishermen in boats, and killed for oil.

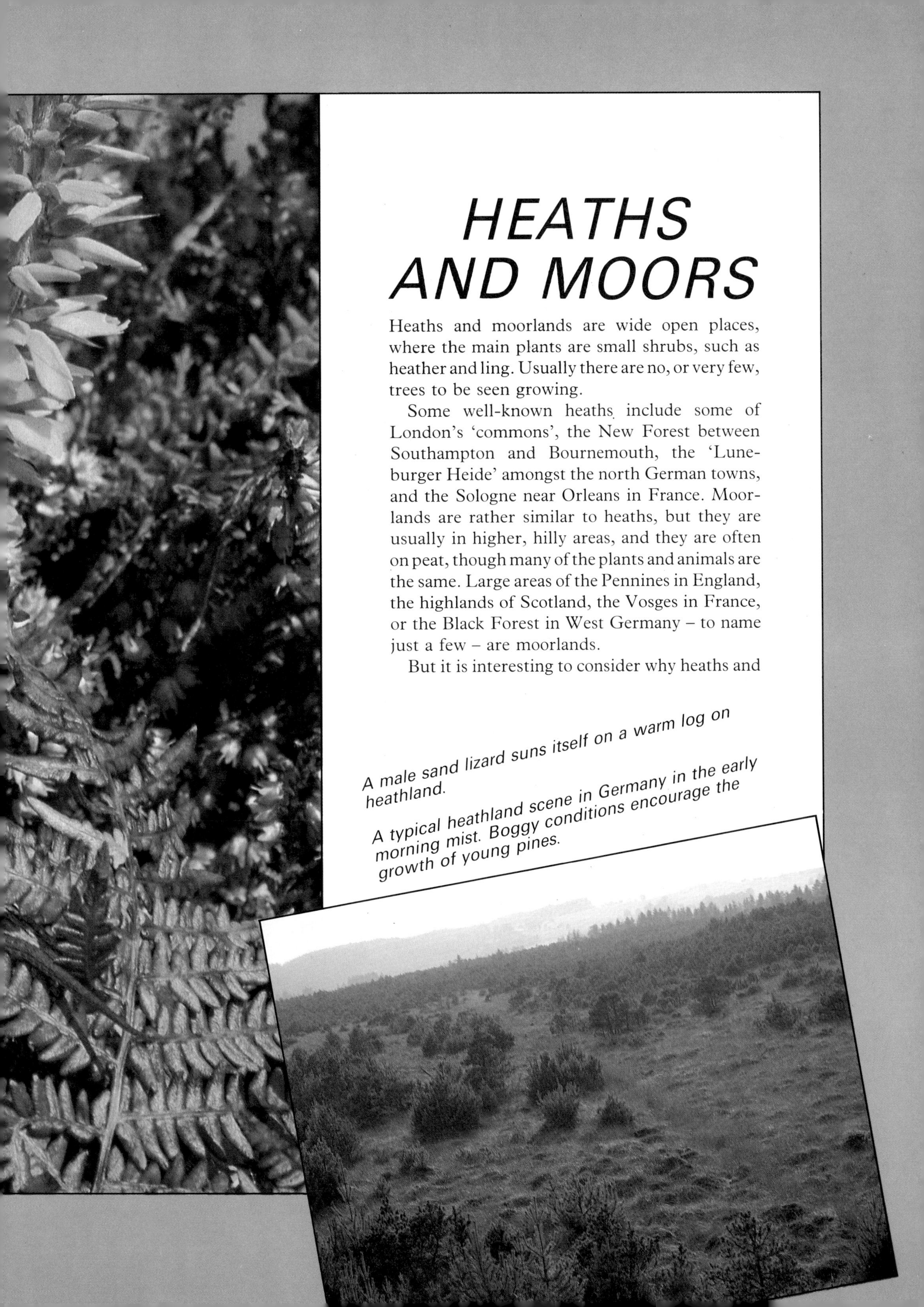

HEATHS AND MOORS

Heaths and moorlands are wide open places, where the main plants are small shrubs, such as heather and ling. Usually there are no, or very few, trees to be seen growing.

Some well-known heaths include some of London's 'commons', the New Forest between Southampton and Bournemouth, the 'Luneburger Heide' amongst the north German towns, and the Sologne near Orleans in France. Moorlands are rather similar to heaths, but they are usually in higher, hilly areas, and they are often on peat, though many of the plants and animals are the same. Large areas of the Pennines in England, the highlands of Scotland, the Vosges in France, or the Black Forest in West Germany – to name just a few – are moorlands.

But it is interesting to consider why heaths and

A male sand lizard suns itself on a warm log on heathland.

A typical heathland scene in Germany in the early morning mist. Boggy conditions encourage the growth of young pines.

Above: *The heather and gorse-covered slopes of sandy heathland by the coast in Dorset, southern England.*

moorlands exist at all, for the natural vegetation over much of Europe is woodland. Why aren't the heaths and moorlands covered in trees, looking like woodland? The answer, as with so many of our 'natural' habitats, is that man has had a hand in the way they have developed, and heaths were really something quite different until man came along.

After the last ice age, just about the whole of north-west Europe, except the highest mountains, became covered with forest of one sort or another. This included the areas that are now heathland. However, in prehistoric times, particularly in the Bronze Age and Iron Age, man was busy making clearings in the forest, at first just to make places where he could persuade wild animals to congregate, but later for ploughing or deliberate pasture. On the more acid rocks, like sands and gravels, the fertile ground that lay below the original woodland cover was quickly washed away, and the soil changed, making it less suitable for pasture, and more suitable for heather. The process continued gradually until the heathers dominated and the land became what we now call heathland.

Many moorlands have formed in the same way. Those high wind-swept moorland areas were once covered with trees, which may have been pretty stunted, admittedly, at higher levels. But it was the effects of man using fire, axes and grazing animals, that turned them into moorlands, though there are also natural moorland areas above the tree-line (*See Mountains*).

HEATHLAND MANAGEMENT

However, it is not quite this simple. You may have noticed that some areas which have 'heath' as part of their name are now covered by birch, oak, or other trees. This is because heathlands cannot maintain themselves, and if you leave them alone, they gradually turn into woodland, just like a meadow does. Many of them have lasted until now because they were once considered to be much more useful places, and were grazed by cattle or sheep, cut for bedding material, or burnt to improve the grazing. As a result the areas remained heathland rather than changing back into woodland. Nowadays, heathland rarely fits into the local farming pattern, and apart from a few exceptions such as the Luneburger Heide which is grazed by sheep, or the New Forest heaths, which are grazed by ponies and cattle, it is neither managed nor grazed. This means that much so-called heathland is gradually disappearing under woodland.

Above: *Red grouse, like the family here, typically inhabit upland heather moors.*

Below: *A view in the Scottish Highlands showing the pattern of heather burning on the grouse moors.*

HEATHLAND AND MOORLAND LIFE

Because the vegetation of heaths and moorland is often dominated by just the one plant – heather – it leaves little scope for insect life to breed and feed, few places for birds to nest, and a limited choice of cover or food for mammals to use. Both heaths and moors are very low in nutrients and lime, because it has all leaked out of the soil, so they tend to be rather unproductive, slow-growing places.

This means, however, that such life as there is, is quite interesting or rare, because it has developed special ways of coping with the poor environment.

The commonest plants of heathland are heathers and ling. They are able to thrive because they are adapted to the dry, sandy soil. The roots spread out widely only a short distance below the surface so that they are able to absorb rain-water easily. Most of the other species on a heath also have shallow root systems. Bracken is also common and in many places it may be so plentiful that it kills the heather. There may also be small flowering plants such as ivy leaved bellflower and heath speedwell on the moors.

The heather provides food for certain wild animals. Mountain hares depend upon it and it is also grazed by red deer. On some moors, short-tailed voles are plentiful. Short-eared owls, harriers and red grouse also depend on the heather for their food.

Heaths are also wonderful places for insects. Heath and mottled grasshoppers bask on bare sandy areas and fall prey to small birds and sand lizards. Smooth snakes and adders also love sunny, dry heaths and are active predators of lizards and birds. Early spring, when they have just woken from hibernation, is the best time of year to see these reptiles as they bask in the sun.

Bird-life and moorland management

In many areas of moorland, especially in northern Britain, the heather moors are managed especially with red grouse in mind. When it was discovered that grouse particularly like the young growths of heather, in preference to older heather, a special way of management was devised – by burning. The burning is most successful if carried out when the heather is between 10 and 15 years old, so a carefully organized programme of burning was worked out. Under this scheme, the moorlands look like a sort of patchwork, with little bits being burnt here and there, with no single bit being burnt more than once in about 12 years.

The densities of grouse on these patchworks, are much higher on the young areas. During the breeding season, the male grouse also defend much smaller territories, presumably because they know that they can obtain enough food from a smaller area for themselves and their young. Interestingly, other animals, such as the mountain hare, will also vary in density according to the age of the heather.

This is why some hills in Scotland and elsewhere look so strange, with their chequerboard effect – and it explains why parts of them may still be smouldering!

Above: *An intricate dew-covered web of an orb-web spider on a heath in autumn.*

PROJECT

A heathland profile

The best way to look at a heathland soil is to find a new gravel pit, road-cutting, or a bank where there has been a small land-slip, exposing a section down through the soil. You can dig your own small pit, as soil scientists do, but you will need to check if this is allowed. What you should see will vary according to the original soil type, and the age of the heathland, amongst other things.

At the top will be a layer of plant debris, beginning to rot down. Below this is a layer which has had all the minerals removed from it by the acid rainfall percolating through, and this layer may look like white ash. A little further down, where the water has slowed, the minerals are redeposited in a reddish layer, and sometimes this forms into a rock-hard layer known as an iron pan. Not surprisingly, this iron pan just below the surface makes it difficult for larger plants to grow as their roots struggle to grow down through it, and so it plays a part in maintaining heathland.

If you find a good profile, work out how many layers there are in the profile and draw them.

DEPENDENT HABITATS

One reason that heaths are often more rewarding to visit than you might expect is because they are often part of a system that includes other habitats, expecially bogs, pools, and wet heathland. In places where the underground water level comes close to the surface and even allows pools of water to form on it, the heath becomes wet and other species of plant may be seen. Unlike bogs in fields, heathland bogs receive a nice, even supply of unpolluted water that is low in nutrients, and contains hardly any mud. The combination of heath and bog is ideal for wildlife. Dragonflies, for example, will emerge from the bogs, hunt over heathland, and some of them will get snapped up by the hobbies. Snakes and lizards can move on to the drier heathland in spring and autumn, but they can retreat to the damper boggy areas if it gets too hot, or if a fire sweeps through the heath.

Watch out for bright-green areas amongst the heathland – this green colour is sphagnum moss, and indicates where the bogs will be. But take care when investigating them; some are very deep.

Around the Mediterranean, there is a rather different sort of heathland that has developed in the much drier climate of that area. Many more flowers appear here in spring, before the droughts of summer than on northern heaths.

A male emperor moth on heather, displays the false 'eyes' on its hind wings.

This heathland appears in two main forms: maquis and garrigue. The maquis is usually the densest vegetation, often growing as high as 2 metres, and covering most of the ground surface, like a dwarf forest. It is dominated by plants like broom and tree-heather. Garrigue is much more open, with just scattered low bushes; it usually grows in the very hottest and driest hillsides.

An adder, common in dry heathlands, basks on a log in the late summer sunshine.

Insect-eating plants

Most people know that there are insect-eating plants in the tropics, such as the Venus' flytrap, but did you know that we have quite a few different insect-eating plants in north-west Europe? By far the best place to see them is in bogs amongst heathlands. This is almost certainly because bogs are so poor in nutrients that any plant growing there needs a little extra to survive. They obtain these vital nutrients from the bodies of insects and other tiny creatures which they catch.

None of them catch insects in a dramatic way, by snapping shut on them, but they are all fascinating to watch. The main sorts are the sundews, the butterworts, and the bladderworts, and each works in a rather different way to catch its prey.

Sundews have sticky bright red hairs on their leaves, covered with a glue-like substance. When an unfortunate insect lands on a leaf, its legs and wings immediately get trapped, and it is unable to fly or walk away. Only the strongest insects, such as large dragonflies, or wasps, can escape, and even butterflies are often caught. The sundew's leaf curls slightly over the trapped insect, and digesting enzymes are produced by the plant, turning the insect into a sort of soup, allowing it to be absorbed by the leaf.

The butterworts work in a rather similar way, but their leaves do not have sticky hairs. They are just sticky all over, and can fold in over an insect, only catching much smaller, weaker insects.

The bladderworts are quite different, yet most of them still grow in boggy areas or bog pools. They are aquatic plants, with leaves that lie below the water level, occasionally sending up a spike of beautiful yellow or orange flowers. The underwater leaves have little bladders on them, each with a tiny trigger; when passing a water-flea or similar little creature touches the trigger, a 'trapdoor' opens, taking a rush of water – plus the insect – into the bladder. Once in there, it has no means of escape, and it gradually gets digested like the ones on the leaves of the other plants.

*Boggy conditions in moors and heaths encourage a typical mixture of insect-eating plants including butterwort (*right*) and sundews (*centre left*).*

Main picture: *Garrigue, in the hot dry mountainside bordering the Mediterranean, in southern France.*

Below: *Cowberry, a member of the heath family. Its leaves are evergreen and it has a bright red berry.*

Bottom: *Bilberry is a close relation of the cowberry, but it sheds its leaves in autumn. Before they fall they change through a wonderful range of colours.*

Tormentil ht 15–30 cm
Potentilla erecta. Attractive trailing plant, with 4-petalled flowers throughout summer and autumn. Common on heaths and moors throughout north Europe.

Bilberry ht 15–30 cm
Vaccinium myrtillus. Familiar plant of heaths and moors, best known for its edible blue-black berries, that occur in abundance in late summer. Green and red flowers, in early summer, are often overlooked. Common and widespread.

Bell heather ht up to 40 cm
Erica cinerea. More colourful, and with larger flowers, than ling. Bell heather almost as common in similar places, though prefers drier parts of heaths and moors, where may also become dominant.

Dodder ht 10–60 cm
Cuscuta epithymum. Unusual plant, that is wholly parasitic on other plants, drawing all its nourishment from them, so needs no green colour of its own. Pink stems, trailing over heather or gorse, are familiar site on heaths and moors.

Heath speedwell ht 15–30 cm
Veronica officinalis. Low creeping plant that sends up spikes of attractive blue flowers. Flowers from May to July, and occurs in heathy places throughout.

Cross-leaved heath ht 10–50 cm
Erica tetralix. Another heather that occurs on heaths and moors, but usually confined to wetter parts. Flowers are paler pink than bell-heather, and are clustered at top of greyish stems.

Ling ht 10–50 cm
Calluna vulgaris. Also called heather. One of commonest and most familiar heathland plants, often dominating large areas, giving rise to name 'heathland'. Flowers in late summer, and widespread throughout north-west Europe.

SHRUBS

Gorse ht 1–1.5 m
Ulex europaeus. One of most familiar plants, well-known for spiny impenetrable bushes, and masses of yellow flowers in early spring. Common on heaths and grassy areas throughout western parts of Europe.

Broom ht 60 cm–2 m
Sarothamnus scoparius. Similar to gorse, but with no spines, and larger more attractive flowers, in early summer. Bushes are familiar sight on heaths and acid grasslands throughout western Europe.

INSECTS AND OTHER INVERTEBRATES

Silver-studded blue ws 24–30 mm
Plebejus argus. Commonest small blue butterfly on heaths and similar areas, but looks like many other species. Main caterpillar food-plants are gorse and broom, both common on heaths.

Fox mouth ws 40–65 mm
Macrothylacia rubi. Orangey-brown males fly by day on heaths and moors, though the greyer females are nocturnal. Common and widespread throughout western Europe. Larvae are velvety black with orange rings.

Mottled grasshopper bl 12–19 mm
Myrmeleotettix maculatus. Small but distinctive grasshopper, that occurs in open areas on warm heathland. Call sounds like old-fashioned watch being wound up! Common in suitable habitats throughout, except in far north.

Sand wasp bl 14–24 mm
Ammophila sabulosa. One of several large red and black solitary wasps found in sandy heathland areas. Female lays eggs in burrows, which she stocks up with live caterpillars. Widespread and reasonably common.

Emperor moth ws 55–65 mm
Saturnia pavonia. Conspicuous large, colourful and day-flying. Occurs on heathland and other open habitats through most of Europe. Flies in spring. Males most often seen as they search for females.

Grayling butterfly ws 42–50 mm
Hipparchia semele. Common throughout Europe except north, preferring heathy areas and sandy coastal areas. Difficult to see when it settles, as it usually keeps its wings closed together.

Green tiger beetle bl 12–16 mm
Cicindela viridis. Although beautiful metallic green when seen closely, this beetle is surprisingly inconspicuous when settled or in flight. Lives in sandy areas throughout western Europe. Larvae have little burrows in sand, where they wait for prey.

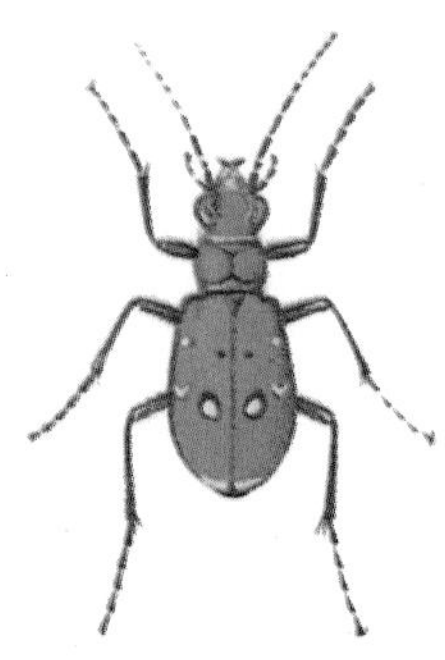

Velvet ant bl 10–14 mm
Mutilla europaea. Not an ant, though related to ants and wasps. So-called because female is velvety and wingless, looking like a large ant. Parasitic on bumble bees, mainly in heathy areas, throughout, but never common.

AMPHIBIANS AND REPTILES

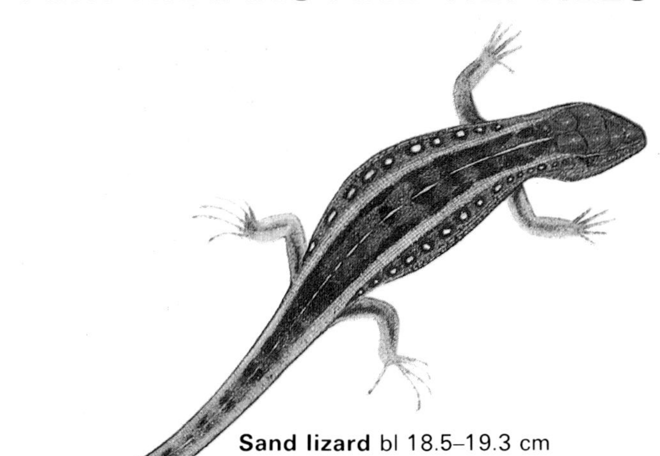

Natterjack toad bl 6 cm
Bufo calamita. Distinctive but small toad with yellow stripe down back. Breeds in warm pools on heathland and dunes over northern Europe, and a wider habitat range further south. Runs, rather than walks.

Sand lizard bl 18.5–19.3 cm
Lacerta agilis. Attractive and brightly coloured, at least in the male, though surprisingly hard to spot. Mainly on heaths and dunes in the north of its range, more widely in the south. Rare in Britain.

Common lizard bl 10–16 cm
Lacerta vivipara. Most abundant lizard in western Europe, occurring in great variety of habitats, wherever there is sunshine to bask in and cover to hide in.

Smooth snake bl 56–65 cm
Coronella austriaca. Uncommon and elusive, found mainly in warm heathland areas, and other sunny, dry situations, throughout central Europe, though rare in Britain. Not venomous.

Adder bl up to 60 cm
Vipera berus. Common and widespread snake, occuring in variety of habitats throughout western Europe. Although venomous, its bite is rarely fatal to humans. Zig-zag pattern helps distinguish it from non-venomous snakes.

Meadow-pipit bl 14.5 cm
Anthus pratensis. Typical 'small brown bird', best distinguished by thin high call, and preference for wild moorland where little else occurs. Common throughout, on heaths and moors.

Stonechat bl 12.5 cm
Saxicola torquata. Conspicuously marked little bird, announcing its presence in the breeding season by loud cracking call, sounding like two stones being hit together. Breeds widely, though rarely commonly, in heathy areas throughout, except Scandinavia.

Twite bl 13.5 cm
Acanthis flavirostris. Similar to linnet, but less colourful, and much more northern and upland in its distribution, breeding in Scotland and across Scandinavia on upland moors. Some migrate south in winter, while others remain.

Hobby bl 30–36 cm
Falco subbuteo. Perhaps the most dashing falcon, catching prey of dragonflies, other insects, and birds (e.g. swallows) on the wing by chasing them. Summer breeding visitor to virtually all of Europe, except further north.

Short-eared owl bl 38 cm
Asio flammeus. Distinctive, because of its daytime hunting habits, and preference for living in open country, such as heaths, moors and dunes. Widespread, especially in north.

Nightjar bl 27 cm
Caprimulgus europaeus. Mysterious evening and night-time bird, rarely seen but often heard either 'churring' from a branch, or clapping its wings at dusk. Widespread in heathy places in south of western Europe, but declining.

Wheatear bl 14.5 cm
Oenanthe oenanthe. White rump is most noticeable feature. Breeds commonly in all sorts of open habitats, especially moors and heaths, throughout Europe. Summer breeding visitor only.

Red grouse bl 32–41 cm
Lagopus iagopus. Red grouse (in UK) and Willow grouse (mainland Europe) are now considered one species, with minor differences. Common on moorland, or in open scrub, in mountain areas through northern Europe.

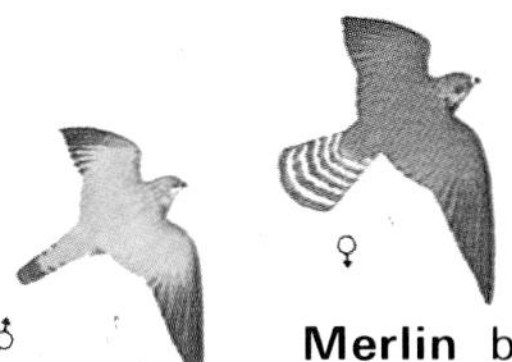

Merlin bl 27–33 cm
Falco columbarius. Smallest European falcon, and most characteristic of moorlands, and uplands. Breeds in such habitats across northernmost Europe, and winters further south throughout.

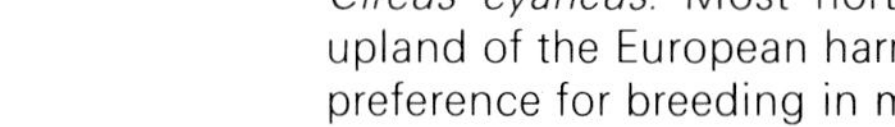

Hen harrier bl 43–51 cm
Circus cyaneus. Most northern and upland of the European harriers, with preference for breeding in moorlands and steppe country. Found in suitable habitats across wilder parts of Europe, spending the winter further south.

Red-backed shrike bl 17 cm
Lanius collurio. Typical shrike, often perching in exposed places, watching for prey. Has declined dramatically in Britain, and parts of range, but still widespread except in the far north. Summer visitor only.

Tree-pipit bl 15 cm
Anthus pratensis. Similar in appearance to meadow-pipit, but different in habits, with preference for perching high in trees and calling, followed by downward fluttering singing flight. Widespread throughout western Europe, but not common anywhere.

Dartford warbler bl 12.5 cm
Sylvia undata. One of the few European resident warblers, remaining all year in an area reaching as far north as south England, and north France. Hard to spot, except when singing in spring.

Linnet bl 13 cm
Acanthis cannabina. Distinctive finch. Male has red forehead and breast. Breeds commonly in heathy places with bushes, except in far north, often in loose colonies.

MOUNTAINS

Mountains are strange things; everyone knows what they are, yet they are very difficult to define accurately. Obviously, the Alps, Pyrenees and Himalayas are mountains, but what about the Black Forest in Germany, or the Pennines in England – are they mountains, or just hills? So much depends on where you are, what other hills are around. In Nepal, there are ranges of mountains reaching to over 3500 metres, but they are called 'hills' there, because the Himalayas next to them are so much higher! In Wales, however, there are peaks of only 500 metres or so that are called 'mountains'.

Certain mountains *are* a good deal higher than their surrounding countryside; they are colder and windier; they are usually steep and often rocky, and they frequently project above the 'tree-line' the level above which trees are unable to grow. Mountains too are often snowy, and colder than their surroundings.

A mountain valley in the Iberian peninsula typically has pine woodland growing on the lower slopes. The golden eagle can sometimes be seen here.

A glaciated valley, showing typical features to be found.

All the mountain areas of central and northern Europe have had glaciers on them in the last 20,000 years, whether there are any there now or not, for we have only just emerged from a great ice age.

The effect that glaciers have on the mountain landscape is tremendous, because their eroding power, over thousands of years, is so great. When you go into a mountain area, you can quickly look around you and identify the features that are caused by glaciation (the former presence of glaciers). In most cases, you can also quickly tell how far down a valley a glacier has travelled, by noticing where the special characteristics stop.

The main things to look for are:

- u-shaped valleys with a broad curved floor, without spurs coming in from each side;
- steep faces on mountain peaks, often with corrie lakes in the hollow at the base of the cliff;
- 'hanging' side valleys, where the erosion of the smaller side valleys was slower, due to the lesser weight of the ice in them compared with the speed at which the glacier deepened the main valley, so they were left hanging high above them;
- regular heaps of material, usually now grassed over, called 'drumlins' that were deposited by the retreating glacier.

ALPINE MEADOWS

The beautiful alpine hay meadow does not quite fit into the altitudinal zone idea. Wherever you go in the Alps, Pyrenees and other mountains, you come across meadows that are brimming over with flowers of all colours, from daffodils and orchids to scabious and oxeye daisies, and they contribute greatly to the beauty of the mountains. Most of these meadows are cut for hay in June and July, and sometimes re-grow in time for another session of flowering before the autumn. These hay meadows are artificial, just like grasslands in the lowlands, in that they are in the zone where there should naturally be forest, and they have been cleared from the forest, often centuries ago.

Because they are usually so old, and their management has been very traditional, they have developed and kept a wonderful array of flowers and insects, many of which are now rare elsewhere. It would not be uncommon to find fifty species, or even more, in a small area.

Higher up the mountains, towards the top of the tree-line, there are often alpine pastures, equally full of flowers. These have usually been cleared from the forest, or at least assisted by heavy grazing of domestic stock, but they are not mown regularly, as most are far too steep. These are the areas where flocks of animals are mainly grazed, keeping the pastures as beautiful flowery swards.

A mass of crocuses growing in a high alpine meadow in spring.

MOUNTAIN ZONES

Mountains can be cold places and as you climb, the temperature falls about 1°C for every 500 metres higher that you go. This means that the summits of the highest mountains will be so cold that they will always be covered in snow. The change of temperature with height will affect the plants that grow there, and several zones will be passed through during a climb up a mountain.

At the bottom of the mountain, plant life is very similar to the surrounding vegetation. As you go up, you often enter a zone of dense forest – this is partly because the clouds tend to drop all their moisture as mist and rain when they rise and cool on hitting the mountainside, which suits the growth of forest perfectly; and partly because the steeper slopes of mountainsides are less suitable for ploughing, so they have been spared clearance for agriculture.

Usually, if you look carefully, you will notice that there is a gradual change in these forests from deciduous trees, such as oak and beech, to coniferous trees, such as spruce, pine and silver fir at the higher altitudes. Try watching out for this next time you drive up a mountain pass, or walk up a mountain.

Above the conifer forests, the trees thin out and get smaller, and there is a zone of stunted open forest, made up of a mixture of trees and shrubs, such as junipers, birches, and dwarfed examples of the upper conifers. This gets smaller still as you go further up, and gives way to a low-growing shrubby moorland, that is naturally treeless. This area, where the trees give way to shrubs and moorland, is known as the 'tree-line', although it is hardly ever a definite line – it depends on aspect, shelter, the soil, and other local factors.

Higher still, if the mountains are big enough, you reach a bare stony tundra-like zone, where there is snow lying for many months of the year. When this melts it exposes damp, frost-shattered rocks and gravelly soil. Surprisingly, many flowers do very well up here, though they are always very small, and this is the place to look for alpine plants, with their dense cushions of flowers and incredibly bright colours. They flower in a

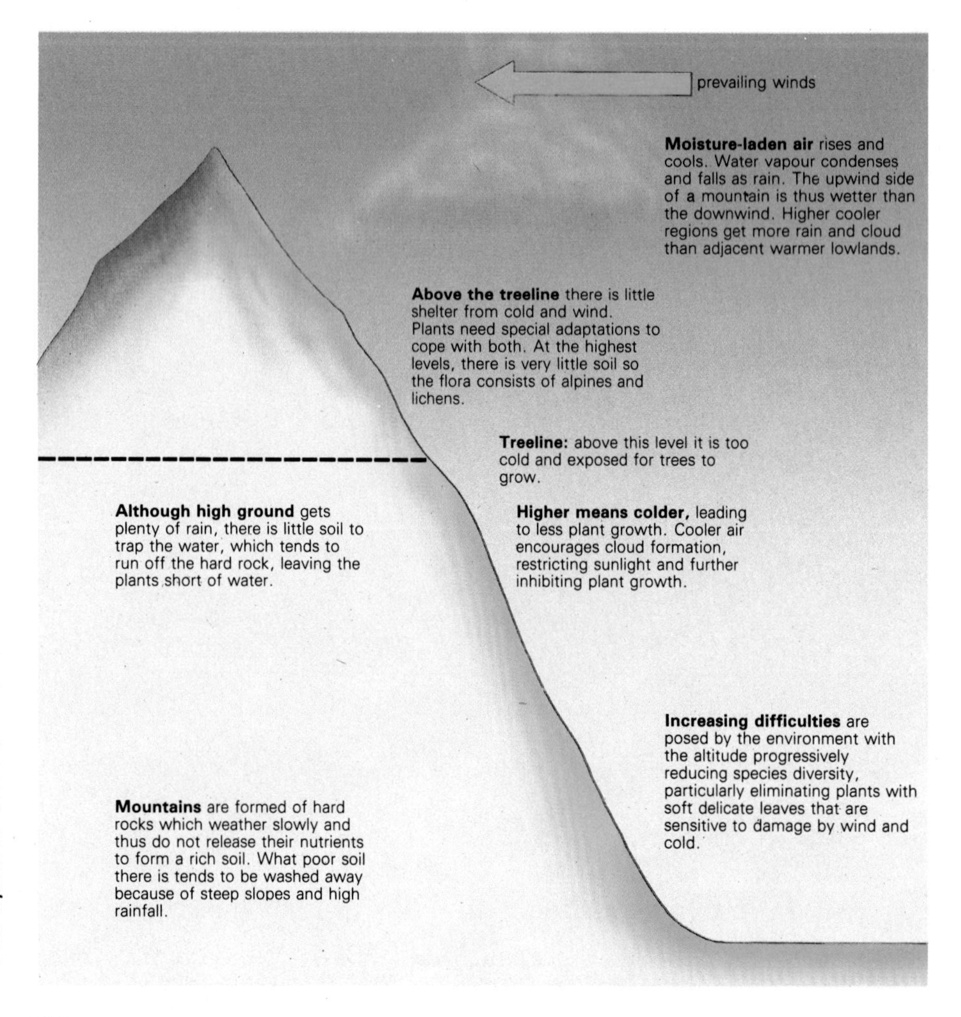

An upland environment.

Right: *The beautiful purple saxifrage grows high on mountains, flowering as soon as the snow melts.*

very short season, from July to early September, between the time that the snows melt and the time that the frosts and snows of autumn return. The first flowers to appear are the charming alpine snowbell which pushes it head through the melting snow. Gentians grow in profusion where even the smallest quantity of soil accumulates. Their blue, trumpet-like flowers contrast with the white petals of mouse-ear. There are also moss campions, alpine anemones and opposite-leaved saxifrage as well as Europe's best known mountain flower, eidelweiss.

Even higher, there may be a zone where only mosses and lichens survive, before you reach the permanent snow-line – the place where the temperature is so low that the snow never melts, whatever the time of year. Up around here, there may be glaciers, cliffs, screes and alpine lakes, cold and inhospitable to all forms of wild life.

Below: *Forests and snowy peaks in the Alps provide a background for rose bay willow herb, which grows on the slopes.*

MOUNTAIN LIFE

The mountains not only support a wealth of plants and animals that have special adaptations to the cold mountain life, but they are also the last refuge for many species, mammals and birds in particular, that used to be widespread but have gone from everywhere else. Mammals, such as the brown bear, the wolf, the lynx and the wildcat, were all quite widespread once but due to changes in their habitats and regrettably, increased hunting, their ranges have constricted. Lynx and bear are now only found in the mountains of Spain and Yugoslavia, although wolf and wildcat have a more extensive range.

The mountain hare is widespread in hills and mountains throughout Britain and Europe. It is perfectly adapted to this harsh environment and in summer its blue/grey fur is a perfect match for lichens and mosses. In winter, however, its coat turns pure white to match the snow. It does not always escape one of its predators, the stoat, which is not fooled by its camouflage. Like the hare, the stoat's fur also turns white in winter when it is known as ermine; only its tail retains any black.

High in the Alps and Pyrenees, chamois haunt rocky crags and slopes. They are superb and fearless climbers and will tackle any incline. They share their habitat with a curious rodent called the alpine marmot. If you venture into its territory, the first thing you will hear is a loud whistle as it alerts its neighbours. Around ski resorts it has often become tame, and will even take food from your hand.

A close-up of a Eyropean lynx, Europe's largest cat.

Above: *A female grey wolf. Only a few European mountain refuges are left to them.*

Left: *An alpine marmot, photographed in high mountain pastures. These shy mammals live in burrows and hibernate during winter months.*

Below left: *The European brown bear, now extremely rare.*

PROJECT ●

Looking at lichens

Lichens are strange plants – a combination of two quite different plants, living together in a close relationship. The result looks unlike either of the two partners, which are always a fungus and an alga, and has special properties not possessed by its components. For example, lichens are able to grow in seemingly very inhospitable places, where there is no soil at all, and they can withstand intense cold. In contrast, most of them are very sensitive to atmospheric pollution, perhaps because they are more dependent on the air than on the soil, and they have gradually disappeared from many polluted areas.

It follows that, with this combination of likes and dislikes, mountains are excellent places for lichens. They do particularly well above the tree-line, right on up to the snow-line, and many boulders at this altitude are totally covered by them.

Lichens grow very slowly, but at a measurable rate each year. You can use them, therefore, to make comparisons of how long different rock surfaces have been exposed. Without further information, you could not work out how many years a rock had been exposed, but – by comparing the size of the largest lichen of the same species – you could estimate that one rock had been exposed for twice as long as another. This has been used to calculate such things as the rate of retreat of glaciers, exposing new rocks as they go; the age of archaeological monuments and so on. It is surprising what can be worked out from such a small plant!

Above: Mountain or map lichen is a common upland species.

Collecting rocks and minerals

You can collect rocks and minerals almost anywhere, but mountains are particularly good places, because they tend to be made up of harder rocks which are more likely to contain things of interest than the soft newer rocks of much of the lowlands. Also, because mountains are less well-covered by vegetation higher up, it is much easier to see the rocks!

Some areas are particularly good for finding minerals in, while some areas are rather poor. A geological map, libraries and any local help will give you more clues on where to look, though certain regions – such as the Auvergne in France – are known internationally. When going out looking for items of interest in the mountains, take a good solid hammer (preferably a geological one, designed for this purpose), a strong chisel, a rucksack, and a notebook. Most important of all, never go into the mountains without experienced adult supervision and remember to tell someone where you are going.

Don't be tempted to break off or collect a huge bit of rock that you find interesting – it is more difficult to carry, harder to display, and more destructive. Just take enough to show what you want, and leave the rest. If you need to break some off, look for suitable cracks in which you can insert the chisel, or break pieces off with your hammer. Close your eyes just at the moment of impact to prevent splinters going in them.

At home, display your collection in drawers, or on shelves, sticking each piece lightly in position, and mounting a label next to it. Most rocks keep perfectly, though iron pyrites rapidly deteriorates, so it is best to coat it with clear varnish.

Birds, such as the eagles, the magnificent lammergeier, alpine choughs, and many others, have suffered the same fate as the mammals, retreating to the mountains as the lowlands have become too populated, too cultivated, or too polluted.

The ptarmigan, however, is a plump partridge-like bird found *only* in mountain areas. It is widespread and occurs from Scotland to the Pyrenees. Its blue/grey plumage gives it superb camouflage in summer as the female broods her eggs among the lichen. In winter, its plumage turns white, enabling it to blend with the snow. A close view of a ptarmigan reveals its feathered toes which protect it from the cold.

In the Alps and Pyrenees, you will often see small birds pecking around the snow-line and even around ski lifts. These will either be snowfinches which have white flashes on their wings, or alpine accentors, relatives of the familiar dunnock.

When you get to the highest parts of mountains, there are still a remarkable number of butterflies, considering the cold climate and the strong winds. One noticeable feature of many of them is that they are quite dark like the sooty ringlet or the mountain ringlet, and where a species occurs right from the lowlands to the highlands, it is often darker in colour at the higher altitudes. It is well known that a dark cuticle absorbs heat better than a light one, so it is probably a means of helping the insects to absorb and keep what little heat there is around. It is certainly not universal, though, since some successful alpine butterflies, like the Apollo or the peak white, are light-coloured or white.

Left: *An Apollo butterfly is one of the most distinctive of alpine species.*

Above: *A pair of common buzzards at their nest in an upland woodland.*

Mountain sorrel ht 25 cm
Oxyria digyna. Mountain relative of the docks and sorrels of the lowlands. Occurs in mountain areas, especially where damp, throughout Europe, though at lower elevations in the north. Flowers in July and August.

Cloudberry ht 18 cm
Rubus chamaemorus. Low creeping blackberry relative, with round shiny leaves, and large solitary white flowers in summer. Later in year, produces orange fruits. Plant of northern moors and mountains.

Mountain avens ht 6 cm
Dryas octopetala. Beautiful mountain and northern plant, that occurs in open limestone areas on mountains, or lower down further north, in Britain and through much of Europe. Flowers in early summer.

Starry saxifrage ht 10 cm
Saxifraga stellaris. Very common plant in wettest places in mountains, by streams and springheads. Rather inconspicuous, as flowers are very small. Occurs throughout western Europe in suitable habitats.

Alpine lady's mantle ht 15 cm
Alchemilla alpina. Frequent plant of mountain grasslands throughout Europe. Its silvery-white leaves, divided to the base, are distinctive. Flowers through summer.

Northern eggar moth
ws 45–75 mm
Lasiocampa quercus callunae. This darker northern form of the eggar moth occurs on hills and mountains through northern Europe, with larvae feeding on heather. Male flies by day, female at night, from early summer onwards

Dewy ringlet ws 38–45 mm
Erebia pandrose. Close relative of the mountain ringlet, but with distinctive greyish marbled underwings. Occurs in mountain areas through most of Europe, and at lower altitudes in Scandinavia. Flies June–August.

Apollo butterfly ws 65–75 mm
Parnassius apollo. Specialized mountain butterfly, occurring in separate populations in most European mountains, up to 2,000 m. Very distinctive colouring, and larger than most similar butterflies.

Small mountain ringlet
ws 30–35 mm
Erebia epiphron. Small, predominantly brown butterfly, found in mountain ranges through Europe except for far north. The British mountain ringlet is a separate subspecies, found locally in Scotland and northern England.

Scotch argus ws 37–48 mm
Erebia aethiops. Larger and more conspicuous than the mountain ringlet, with noticeable eye-spots. Very active in sunshine, but remains hidden in dull weather. Mountains through central Europe. Flies in late summer.

Golden plover bl 27 cm
Pluvialis apricarius. Beautiful medium-sized wader, wintering on coasts, but breeding mainly in mountain areas, and northern moorlands. Call is a melancholy whistle, a characteristic moorland sound in summer.

Ptarmigan bl 35 cm
Lagopus mutus. High-altitude version of red grouse, always found well above the tree-line. Plumage changes in winter, to maintain camouflage. Northern Europe, and mountains further south.

Dotterel bl 23 cm
Eudromius morinellus. Winters on the coast, but breeds in high mountain areas, including Scotland, and far north of Europe. Well-known as a tame species in summer. Call is distinctive thin whistling trill.

Golden eagle bl 75–86 cm
Aquila chrysaetos. Probably the most familiar and majestic bird of prey. Like peregrines, not a mountain specialist, but has retreated to mountains through human pressure. Widespread through wilder and higher parts of Europe.

Snow bunting bl 16 cm
Plectrophenax nivalis. The whitest of buntings. Males almost all-white in breeding season. Breeds in mountain areas and northern tundra, throughout north Europe, though moves south to coasts in winter.

Ring-ouzel bl 24 cm
Turdus torquatus. A mountain equivalent of the familiar blackbird, with a marked white crescent on the chest. Occurs in rocky and mountain areas throughout northern Europe, and in high mountains further south.

Buzzard bl 50–56 cm
Buteo buteo. Resembling eagles, and often confused with them. More rounded wings and tail, and smaller than eagles. Much more common than any eagle. Widespread throughout in mountains and lower areas.

Feral goat size varies widely
Capra hircus. Herds of domesticated goats have gone wild in some areas, usually in mountainous country or on wilder islands. Usually have more white than real wild goats or the ibex, with more spiralled horns.

Short-tailed vole bl up to 13 cm
Microtus agrestis. Although not a mountain specialist, occurs very widely in mountain areas, all over Europe, well above the tree-line. Active all the year.

Wildcat bl up to 65 cm
Felis sylvestris. Confined to mountains in northern Europe (Alps, Scotland), though more widespread further south. Larger than most domestic cats, wilder and fiercer, with marked rings on its tail.

Mountain hare bl up to 60 cm
Lepus timidus. Northern or mountain equivalent of brown hare, occurring up to the arctic and to very high altitudes in Alps. Coat turns white in winter and grey-brown in summer, maintaining its camouflage all year round.

Red deer bl up to 260 cm
Cervus elaphus. Distinguishing mark is a pale rump patch, never white. Gregarious in behaviour. Large herds found in open country, small groups in woodland.

CITIES, PARKS AND GARDENS

Cities, parks and gardens hardly sound like the most promising of wildlife habitats, yet the majority of us live here, after all, so it is the wildlife of such areas that we see the most. So, what is the wildlife of our urban areas like? Is there anything to be found amongst all that concrete and tarmac?

The answer to the second question is an unequivocal 'yes' – the wildlife of urban areas is prolific and varied, and in some surprising ways it has advantages over the wildlife of the countryside. Of course, not all plants and animals can adapt to town life, especially creatures that need large areas of wild countryside – it is difficult, for example, to imagine wildcats, lynx, golden-eagles or lammergeiers colonizing cities. However, it is remarkable what can occur in urban areas, and new species are adapting to the 'good life' all the time.

Cities provide an amazing amount of green space and important wildlife habitat. Robins are a popular and common city habitant.

TOWN AND CITY LIFE

First, let's take a quick look at what the city life has to offer, despite its limitations. Cities, first of all, are warm places, often much warmer than the surrounding countryside. Birds, such as starlings and pigeons, have discovered this, and they have moved into the cities to roost in some places in spectacular numbers. Secondly, they are places where there is a good all-year-round supply of food; the by-products of civilization, in the form

of rubbish and surplus food, are produced all the time, and are available for wildlife to find and eat. Many city-dwellers also deliberately put out food for birds and mammals in winter, and our gardens are cultivated to provide a longer season of flowers, fruit and vegetables than anything in the wild. Thirdly, and perhaps most surprisingly, towns and cities are often less polluted than much of the countryside. Highly industrial areas, it is true, can be quite bad, but residential areas are often much cleaner than farmland, because no pesticides are sprayed from the air, and inorganic fertilizers do not pervade everything. Some bee-keepers even prefer to keep their bees in towns, rather than risk the dangers of the farmed countryside!

Cities offer a wide variety of micro-habitats. There are no large ancient woodlands (though there are often smaller ones, and large ones can occur surprisingly close to cities), no open downlands, no wild moorland, and no heath and bog in most towns or cities. But there are parks, masses of gardens, canals, railway lines and sidings, old industrial land left to go wild, ponds and streams and quite often riversides. The list is endless.

Above: *A male blackbird bringing food to his nestlings in a garden nest.*

Left: *A city park in spring, with crocuses and daffodils in flower and all the trees in blossom.*

GARDEN LIFE

Gardens can be excellent places to look for a wide variety of wildlife, especially birds and insects. Most gardens have a tree or two, or perhaps a hedge, in which birds nest and feed on insects and in which mammals, such as squirrels and mice, breed and hibernate. Lawns may appear rather dull, but even the greenest lawn has earthworms and other invertebrates underneath it, providing food for birds such as starlings and thrushes, and a flowery lawn has an even greater variety of wildlife. Some gardens have a pond which can provide the focal point for masses of wildlife – birds and mammals which come to drink and feed, breeding frogs, toads and newts, dragonflies and many other insects, lots of different flowers, and much more. In most countries, the area covered by gardens is much bigger than that covered by nature reserves, so they become an important reserve for wildlife.

It is well-worthwhile thinking about how a garden can be looked after in a way that will encourage wildlife, and sometimes it may even

Minibeasts is the name given to small invertebrates such as those shown here. A huge number may be found hiding in the neatest lawn and be easily caught.

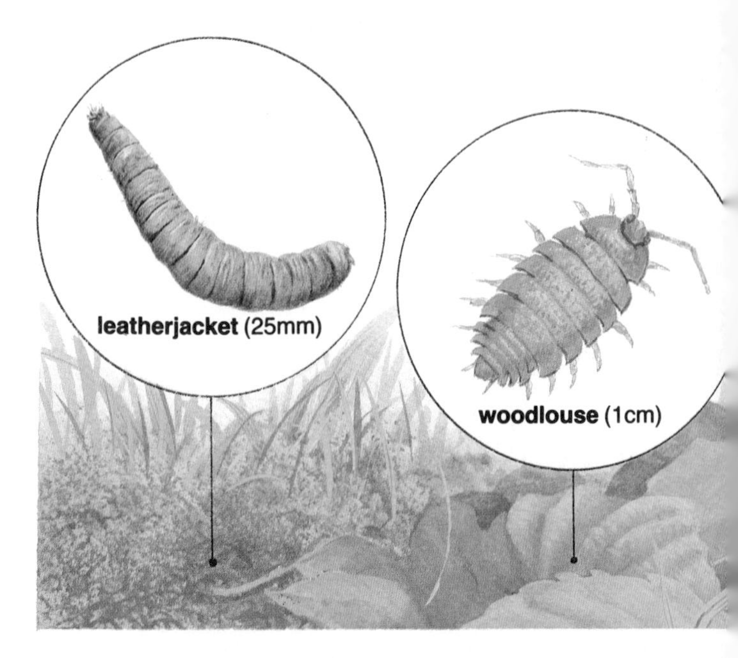

save you and your family work. For example, if you stop putting weedkiller and fertilizer on the lawn, it will gradually become more flowery, and attract more insects and birds; if you leave some of the dead-heads of flowers that contain seeds, you will attract more birds in the autumn and early winter to feed on them. If you need any new trees or shrubs, choose those that will produce fruit suitable for birds, such as *Pyracantha*, or crab-apples, and more birds will visit in winter.

Insects need looking after and attracting too. Virtually all of them are harmless, and many of them are beautiful, and they can do a lot of good by pollinating flowers, attacking the worst pest species, and providing food for insect-eating birds. Try and make sure that your flower beds have plenty of nectar-rich flowers (use a good book on wildlife gardening to help). Also try to persuade your family to give up using insecticides – this will allow natural predators, such as ladybirds, to control the aphids – and plant a few wild plants amongst the exotic garden ones, to allow more insects to breed. You will be surprised at the difference these little changes can make. There are

Gardens can be made into miniature wildlife habitats.

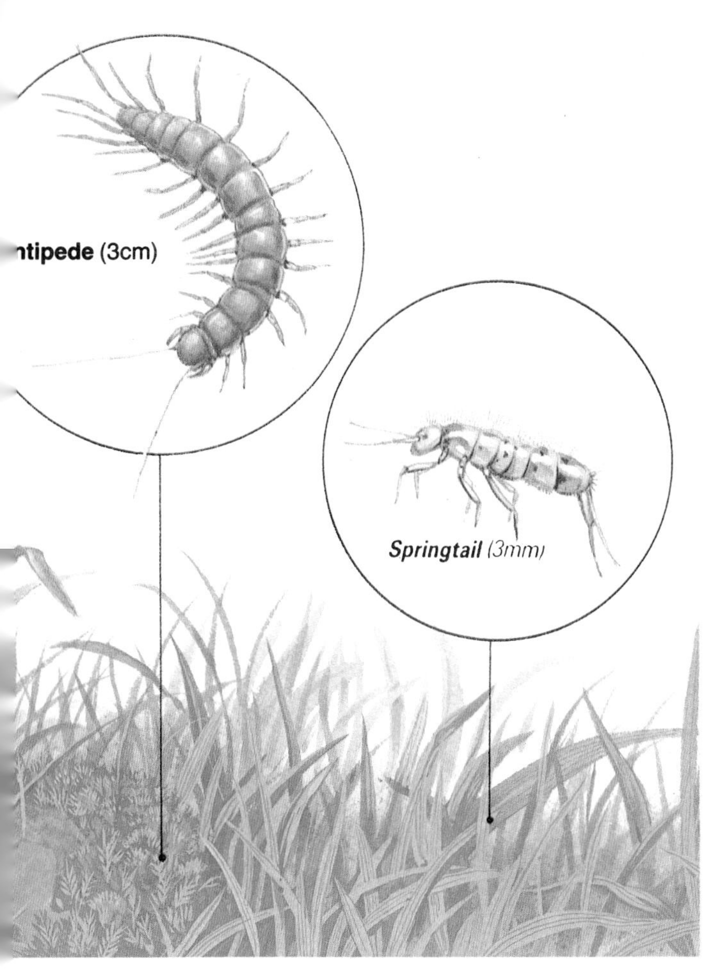

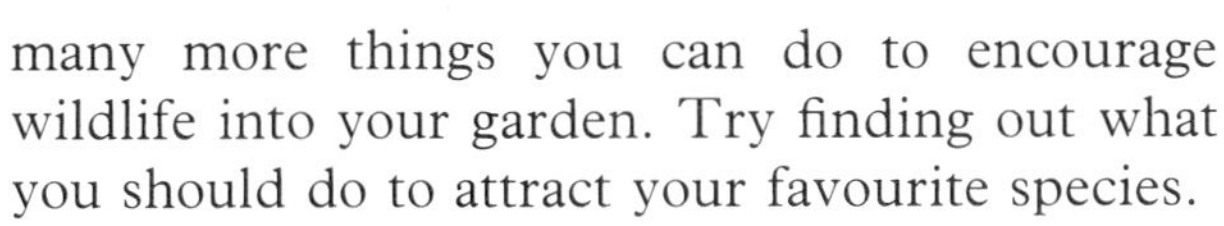

many more things you can do to encourage wildlife into your garden. Try finding out what you should do to attract your favourite species.

A housemartin – one of the most familiar urban birds – at its nest under the eaves of a house.

PROJECT

Making a hedgehog home

Hedgehogs are regular visitors to gardens at night, looking for slugs and other appetizing meals, or coming to eat food put out by the garden owners.

You can encourage hedgehogs to set up home, and even rear young, in your own garden, by making them a suitable home. It will help to attract them to stay if you can leave a little wild corner, and generally have plenty of trees and bushes in the garden, too.

First, find or make a wooden box of about 50 cm × 40 cm × 40 cm such as those used for storing fruit and vegetables. At one end, cut out a hole about 10 cm square, and join this up to an entrance tunnel of similar dimensions, about 20–30 cm long. Then place the box, open side down, in a suitable spot in the garden, such as under a tree or close to a hedge. Drape some strong waterproof polythene, or other suitable waterproof material over the box and then cover it over with soil, leaves, wood, or whatever is to hand to insulate the chamber as well as hiding it. Leave the entrance clear, of course, and wait for signs of activity.

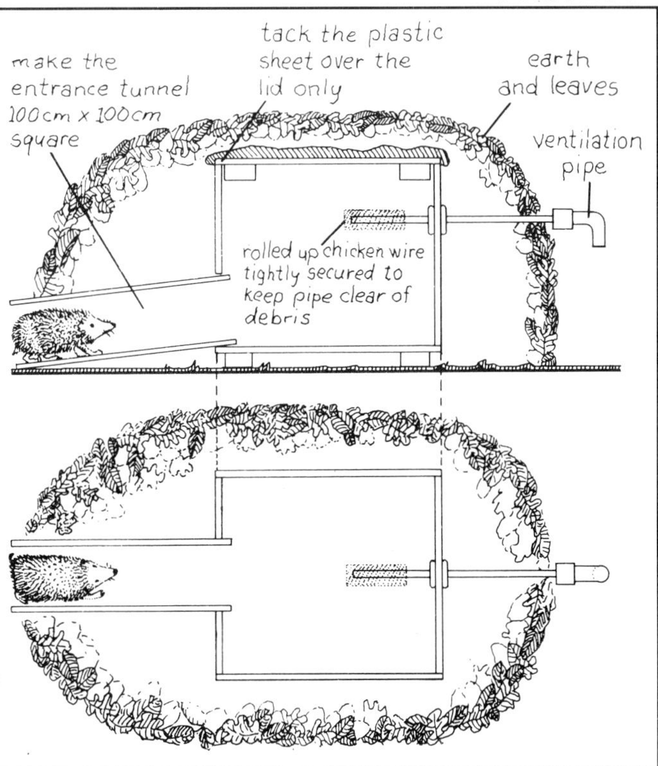

A CLOSER LOOK AT WEEDS

Have you ever thought what makes one plant a weed, and another one not? It can't just be that weeds are unattractive, because some beautiful plants, like rosebay willowherb, are called weeds, so it must be something else. One of the best ways of describing a weed is 'a plant that is growing where it is not wanted'. This means that a plant can be a weed in one place, such as a garden vegetable plot, where it is not wanted, but not be a weed on an old piece of urban wasteland, where it covers the rubbish and looks beautiful.

In fact, had you ever thought that you could get rid of all the weeds in your garden in one go, just by deciding that you like them? Most gardeners would probably not be convinced by this argument, but there is a good case for keeping some weeds, especially because all the native plants of an area – and they are the ones usually considered as weeds – are the best for supporting insect life. Rosebay willowherb, for example, is a most attractive flower, and it is also the food-plant of the caterpillars of the elephant hawk-moth, extraordinary looking things that turn into beautiful moths. The flowers are also very attractive to hoverflies, bees and other nectar-seeking insects.

In fact, rosebay willowherb is an interesting plant to look at, wherever it grows. It is well known as a plant that appears on derelict land, bomb-sites or areas where there has been a fire, and in some places it is known as 'fireweed'. Its success lies in the fact that it can spread rapidly to establish itself on these new sites before they are built on or colonized by other species. It manages this by producing fantastic numbers of wind-borne seeds, that can be carried over long distances, eventually settling on ground well away from the parent plant. Most will settle in unsuitable places, but as long as just a few find a new place where they can grow, then the plant will survive.

Creeping buttercup, one of the most common garden weeds.

Out of interest, try taking a ripe but unopen pod of rosebay seeds, split it onto a tray inside the house (to stop the seeds blowing away), and try to count the number of seeds in it. Multiply this by the number of pods on a plant, and you will see how enormous the number of seeds produced is. This species has a stable population size, (it is becoming neither more common nor rarer) which means that for each plant only one seed is growing into a new plant to replace the original parent. This shows the incredible wastage of seeds.

● PROJECT

PROJECT

Measuring the height of trees

Parks and large gardens are good places to try out some simple ways of measuring the heights of trees, because you can often get well back from single specimens, and have plenty of space to use for the different methods. You do not need special equipment, but you will require the help of a friend.

This method works with any size of tree in open ground. Hold a pencil vertically at arm's length, and move backwards or forwards until you can line up the tree exactly with the top and bottom of the pencil. Carefully turn the pencil sideways so it appears to run along the ground surface, keeping its base at the base of the tree. Ask your friend to walk away from the tree – keeping the same distance from you – until he reaches the spot where the pencil point is. Measure this distance on the ground – and you have the height of the tree.

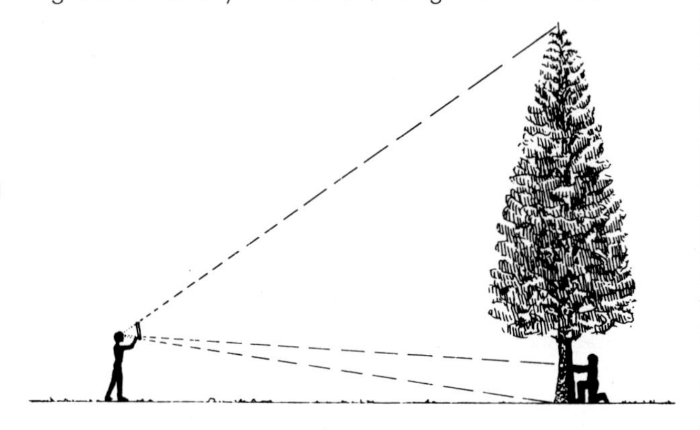

Garden wildlife at night

Most of us only see the garden in the daytime, and we do not realize just what goes on at night outside. You may see a few insects coming to the lighted windows, hear an owl call while you are half-asleep in bed, or wonder what ate the bread you left out, but this does not tell us very much.

One of the most common nocturnal groups of animals is the moths. Almost all moths have adapted to a night-time lifestyle, to avoid being eaten by birds, so we hardly ever see them. From a number of surveys done, it is not uncommon to find 200 or more different species of moth visiting a garden. It would take quite a lot of hard work and experience to record this many, but you can make a start, and perhaps acquire a new interest.

You can buy or borrow specially-made moth traps, which consist of a special bulb, with a net or box around it into which moths fall. You can also try using an ordinary household light, on a long lead, placed outside on a white sheet. Set it up during the daylight in a suitable place where you can be near it, then switch on as night falls. Take a moth guidebook out with you, and go and see what appears. You will find that different moths appear at different times of the night, so the longer you can stay out, the more you will see. The greatest number of moths will appear on a warm, still humid night in summer.

You can also try 'treacling', which involves painting a mixture of molasses, chutney, and a tiny drop of amyl acetate, or a little beer, on posts and tree-trunks. Paint the mixture on before dusk, then watch to see what appears. A warm humid night is needed for treacling to be successful.

A beautiful small elephant hawk moth rests on a butterfly orchid.

Keep your ears alert for sounds, such as bush-crickets calling in dense vegetation; many of them call more at night, and calls are certainly more noticeable then. Bats emit distinctive squeaking sounds which younger people can hear particularly clearly, and you can follow their flight path with your ears. You can also buy or make 'bat-detectors' which amplify the sounds from bats as they seek moths and other large flying insects, using their sensitive sonar system to locate them.

A group of brown, long-eared bats roosting in the loft of a house.

Above: *Common frogs regularly use garden ponds to spawn.*

Below: *A red fox visiting an urban garden.*

● **PROJECT**

PROJECT

Making a pond

A good pond will make your garden, or any other small area of land, more attractive to a range of wildlife. It is not too difficult to make and need not be large.

Select a suitable site, and mark it out with string and pegs. Then, dig the hole so that it shallows towards the edges, but reaches at least 40 cm. (preferably a little more) at some point near the middle. Clear out any sharp stones, then line the hole with fine sand, or old carpet underlay, or even thick newspaper sheets. Buy some polythene or PVC allowing enough to reach down to the deepest part and overlap the edge all the way round. Lay this down so that it lines the hole and begin to fill the pond with water, allowing the liner to settle onto its bedding material. When it is full, complete the edges with turf, stones, or earth. If you can afford it, a double liner is better to guard against leaks. Remember that the thicker, more expensive liners last longer.

Gently put a layer of earth into the bottom of the pond – for plants to root in – then wait a week or

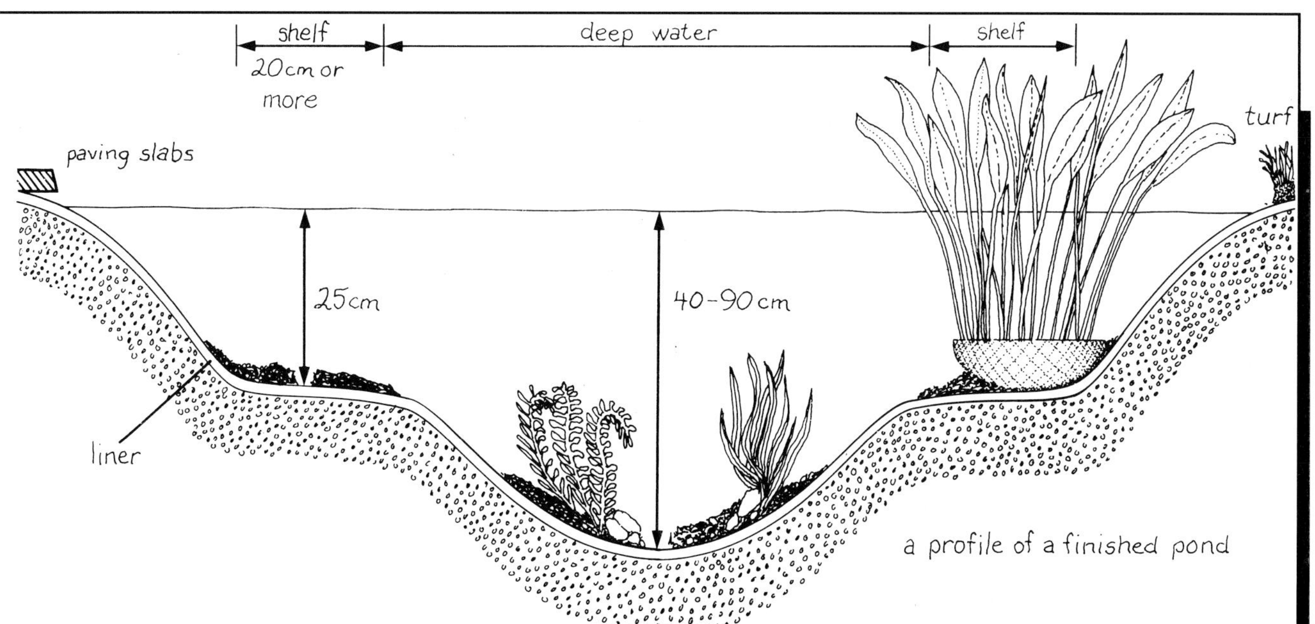

so to allow the water to clear, before introducing a selection of different aquatic plants, both rooting and floating. Gradually introduce water animals from friends' ponds or similar places. Ornamental fish are best avoided – they eat everything!

Your pond will look very mature and settled in a remarkably short space of time, and you will soon attract birds, frogs, newts, and many aquatic insects from all round.

● PROJECT

Making a pitfall trap

When night falls, or under the cover of a dense layer of vegetation, there is much activity that we never see. Many insects are almost entirely nocturnal, partly for reasons of safety, and partly to avoid drying out. These are the ones that we occasionally catch a glimpse of as they scurry away when we lift up a stone or log. They include creatures such as ground beetles, centipedes, some spiders and earwigs.

To get an idea of what is going on at night in your garden, or anywhere else you are interested in, try making some pitfall traps to catch a sample of the creatures that are moving around. These traps are simply straight-sided glass jars, set into the ground into which creatures may fall at night, but from which they are unable to get out because of the smooth glass sides. The jars have to be set so that the rim does not project above the ground, and each one should be covered by a piece of slate, or something similar, raised up two or three centimetres on little stones, to prevent rain from flooding the trap.

Try setting up several traps all over your garden to see if you get different animals in each, but they should be checked and emptied each morning, before the occupants die. Occasionally, you may find some large predator looking well-fed with nothing else to be seen, but this is unusual! Usually, there will be a variety of animals in the trap – beetles, spiders and harvest mice are amongst the most common. A lot depends on the weather, and what the habitat you are studying is like. Try it – it opens the way to a world that is normally unseen.

FLOWERS

Buddleia ht 1–5 m
Buddleia davidii. One of several species of buddleia, all from eastern Asia, that have now become naturalized in waste places, especially around old buildings, in towns and cities. Very attractive to butterflies when in flower, hence its common name of 'butterfly bush'

Hairy bittercress ht 20 cm
Cardamine hirsuta. Common weed, that particularly occurs in cracks in masonry and brickwork. Seeds are dispersed explosively, and come to rest in such cracks, where they germinate. Common throughout.

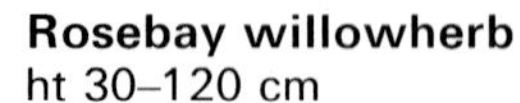

Rosebay willowherb
ht 30–120 cm
Epilobium angustifolium. Abundant and frequent 'weed' of waste places in cities and towns. Its light windborne seeds allow it to colonize any newly bare land very quickly, and soon spreads once there.

Shepherd's purse 8–40 cm
Capsella bursa-pastoris. Abundant and widespread weed of waste places. Small white flowers are inconspicuous, but followed by distinctive fruits that look, fancifully, like a shepherd's purse!

Common bindweed 30–100 cm
Convolvulus arvensis. Several bindweeds occur in urban areas. This is small pinkish one, that creeps over ground, and up walls and fences. Very common throughout in disturbed habitats.

Coltsfoot ht up to 15 cm
Tussilago farfara. Attractive yellow flowers produced very early in spring, well before leaves, coming up in most unlikely places. Large downy leaves appear later in season.

Ground elder 40–100 cm
Aegapodium podagraria. One of the most pernicious and least popular garden weeds, persisting despite any attempts to remove it. If allowed to flower, produces attractive white flower-heads, that are good nectar sources for insects.

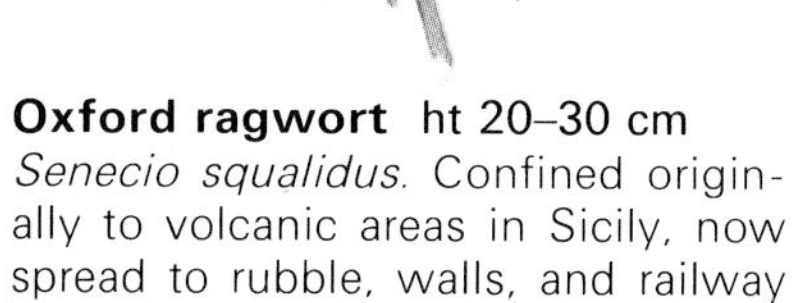

Oxford ragwort ht 20–30 cm
Senecio squalidus. Confined originally to volcanic areas in Sicily, now spread to rubble, walls, and railway lines in towns and cities through much of Britain and France, where is now familiar.

Red valerian ht 30–80 cm
Centranthus ruber. Native only to southern Europe, but has spread through much of northern Europe, from garden introductions, and colonized old buildings, walls and waste ground more widely.

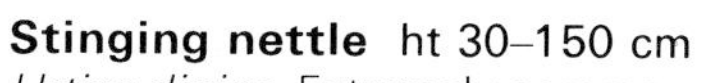

Stinging nettle ht 30–150 cm
Urtica dioica. Extremely common and tenacious weed, well-known for its stinging foliage and stems. Tassles of inconspicuous green flowers. Very useful as main caterpillar foodplant for a number of butterflies. Widespread throughout.

TREES

Plane tree ht up to 35 m
Platanus hybrida. Also known as 'London plane'. Widely planted as attractive street tree throughout central Europe, though origins are unknown. Retains attractive round prickly fruits through the winter.

Sycamore ht up to 35 m
Acer pseudoplatanus. Very common and familiar tree, in towns, gardens and countryside. Originally only native in south-east Europe, but now widely planted and naturalized through most of western Europe. Hardy and pollution tolerant.

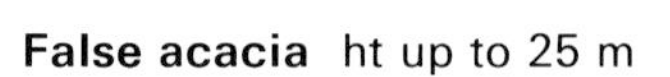

False acacia ht up to 25 m
Robinia pseudacacia. Originally from warmer parts of north America, but planted widely through central and southern Europe, and well-naturalized on dry soils. When in full flower, has very strong scent.

Horse chestnut ht up to 25 m
Aesculus hippocastanum. Well-known for beautiful 'candles' of white flowers in spring, and fruit – 'conkers' – in autumn. Only native in south-east Europe, but very widely planted throughout Europe and occasionally naturalized.

INSECTS AND OTHER INVERTEBRATES

Garden tiger moth ws 50–78 mm
Arctia caja. Common in all sorts of habitats, including gardens, though adults are nocturnal and rarely seen. Better known by its 'woolly bear' caterpillars, often found around towns and gardens.

Garden snail bl 35 mm
Helix aspersa. Hermaphrodite found in hedgerows, waste ground, gardens and on walls. Abundant on chalky soil where there is plenty of calcium to strengthen its shell.

Leaf-cutter bee bl up to 12 mm
Megachile centuncularis. Looks like a broad honey bee. Often nests in holes in rotting wood. Builds brood cells from pieces cut from leaves.

Small tortoiseshell ws 44–50 mm
Aglais urticae. Small brightly-coloured butterfly. Frequent garden visitor, coming to buddleia and other nectar sources, and breeding on stinging nettles. Common throughout western Europe.

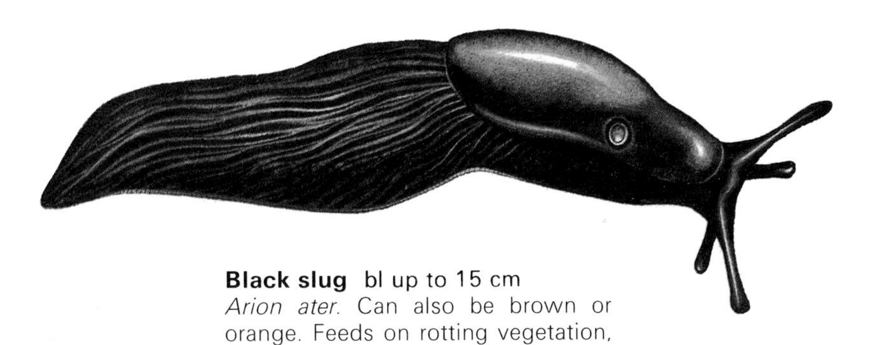

Black slug bl up to 15 cm
Arion ater. Can also be brown or orange. Feeds on rotting vegetation, usually at night and during wet days, as they easily lose moisture from their bodies.

Small white ws 46–54 mm
Pieris rapae. All-too abundant garden visitor. Frequently breeds on garden brassica crops, such as cabbages. Occurs in abundance, throughout the area, during the whole summer.

Peacock ws 54–58 mm
Inachis io. One of the largest and most distinctive butterflies, though surprisingly inconspicuous when it closes its wings. Breeds on nettles, and regularly visits garden flowers for nectar. Common throughout.

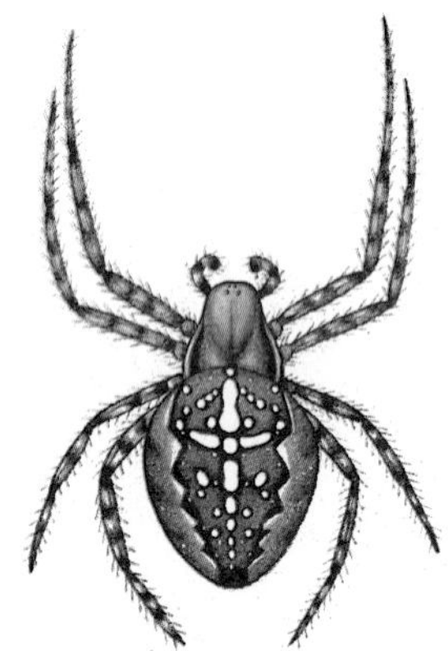

Garden spider
bl 12 mm (female), 8 mm (male)
Araneus diadematus. One of the commonest and most distinctive spiders. In late summer and autumn, females sit on large orb webs, where white cross on their backs is conspicuous. Widespread and common.

Seven-spot ladybird
bl 5.5–7.5 mm
Coccinella 7-punctata. One of the commonest ladybirds around gardens. Both adults and larvae eat aphids, such as greenfly, so are particularly welcome in gardens.

Comma ws 44–48 mm
Polygonia c-album. A butterfly that has extended range greatly in recent years, and is now common visitor to gardens for nectar, and for over-ripe fruit in autumn. So-called because of white crescent on underside of wings.

Eyed hawkmoth bl 80 mm
Smerinthus ocellata. Large and impressive moth, though mainly nocturnal, so not often seen. Feeds on apple trees and willows, and is quite frequent around gardens.

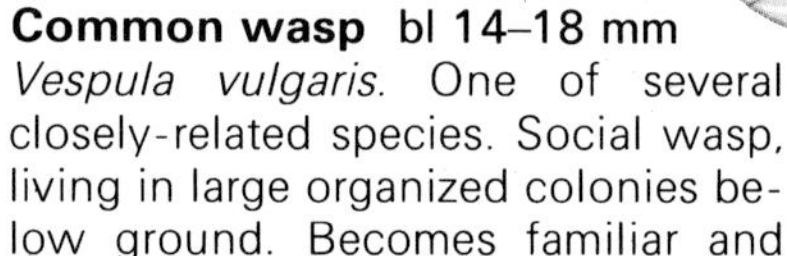

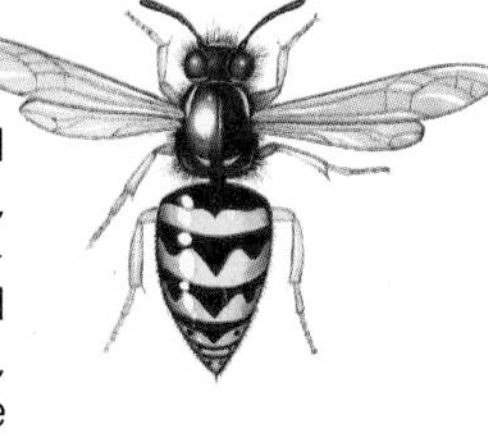

Common wasp bl 14–18 mm
Vespula vulgaris. One of several closely-related species. Social wasp, living in large organized colonies below ground. Becomes familiar and troublesome everywhere in autumn, when eating habits of workers change to seeking out sweet things.

BIRDS

House sparrow bl 14.5 cm
Passer domesticus. Has become associated with man worldwide, and never occurs in any other habitat. Nests in and on buildings, and feeds on by-products of humanity. Common and familiar everywhere.

Song thrush bl 23 cm
Turdus philomelus. Very familiar and common. Breeds regularly in gardens and feeds on snails and other invertebrates. Widespread and common throughout. Song is one of best-loved of birdsongs.

Kestrel bl 32–35 cm
Falco tinnunculus. Only falcon that has readily taken to urban life. Kestrels have benefited from abundance of small mammals in rough grass along motorways and in urban areas, and are now familiar sight everywhere.

Blue tit bl 11.5 cm
Parus caeruleus. Little bird, but familiar because of regular visits to gardens for peanuts and other food, and fearless, acrobatic behaviour. Breeds in gardens, nestboxes or natural holes. Common throughout.

Jackdaw bl 33 cm
Corvus monedula. Common everywhere, but has a particular liking for nesting in old buildings, and is tame enough to use urban parks and gardens for feeding in. Grey head is distinctive feature.

House martin bl 14 cm
Delichon urbica. Very familiar town bird, that has transferred in large numbers from natural cliff habitat to that of houses. White rump, and distinctive nesting place under eaves, make identification easy.

Blackbird bl 25 cm
Turdus merula. Jaunty black-plumaged blackbird, with yellow bill, is one of commonest birds of town and garden (and many other habitats). Frequently becomes very tame, taking food from hand quite readily.

Swift bl 16.5 cm
Apus apus. Almost totally associated with man nowadays, often breeding in buildings. Sickle-shaped wings, acrobatic flight, and screaming call familiar to town-dwellers everywhere, as groups circle around the buildings.

Starling bl 21.5 cm
Sturnus vulgaris. Has taken readily to towns and cities, often roosting in huge numbers in warmth of city centres. When seen close to, plumage is beautifully multi-coloured, though appears drab from a distance. Very noisy.

Collared dove bl 32 cm
Streptopelia decaocto. One of most successful birds of recent times, spreading from Asia right throughout Europe, as resident breeding bird. Insistent cooing is now familiar in towns and villages everywhere.

Black redstart bl 14 cm
Phoenicurus ochruros. Regular nesting visitor in many European towns and cities, extending as far north as Denmark, and including south-east England. Colouring and constantly-flicking red tail make identification easy.

White stork bl 110 cm
Ciconia ciconia. Distinctive and well-known, by virtue of its habit of nesting on chimneys, roofs, and other conspicuous parts of buildings. Has declined greatly, and is gradually retreating eastwards despite protection.

Robin bl 14 cm
Erithacus rubecula. In some countries, especially Britain, exceptionally familiar and tame bird, beloved by everyone. Elsewhere, much wilder. Colour combination, in both sexes, is quite distinctive.

Pied wagtail bl 18 cm
Motacilla alba. Lively bird, familiar in most built-up areas. 'Chissick' call is almost equally well-known. Breeds on buildings everywhere, and is resident through winter, though may often change habitat.

Spotted flycatcher bl 14 cm
Muscicapa striata. Regular summer visitor to the whole area, though one of the latest migrants to arrive. Widespread, though rarely common, throughout Europe, nesting in gardens, parks and elsewhere, often in open-fronted nestboxes.

MAMMALS

Hedgehog bl 20–30 cm
Erinaceus europaeus. Probably most familiar of garden-visiting mammals, and remarkably tame. Common and widespread in towns and gardens, as well as most areas of wooded countryside.

House mouse bl up to 10 cm
Mus musculus. Extremely common and widespread animal, throughout Europe and most of the world. Almost always associated with man, frequently living in houses or outbuildings. Feeds on almost anything, and breeds all year if food is available.

Pipistrelle bat ws 19–25 cm
Pipistrellus pipistrellus. Most common and widespread bat, as well as smallest, in Europe. Frequently seen in towns and gardens as main roost sites are in houses and other buildings, though these are rarely noticed.

Long-eared bat ws 23–28.5 cm
Plecotus auritus. Exceptionally long ears distinguish it from all but very similar grey long-eared bat. Common and widespread throughout western Europe, except far north, roosting regularly in buildings.

Common rat bl 20–28 cm
Rattus norvegicus. One of the most abundant and widespread animals in Europe, though originally introduced from Asia. Very common in most places associated with man, though uncommon in genuinely natural habitats.

Grey squirrel bl 25.5 cm
Sciurus caroliniensis. Introduced North American species now common over most of lowland Britain, though not, as yet, in mainland Europe. Similar habits to the red squirrel, but much more common in deciduous woodlands. Tends to feed more often on the ground.

WATCHING AND CONSERVING

Anyone who is interested in wildlife cannot fail to be interested in conserving and protecting it. Our wildlife and countryside is under so much pressure today, more so than ever before, that it is vital for everyone who does care about wildlife to do something towards helping to conserve it.

In the UK, in many areas, 95% of the flowery meadows have disappeared over the last 40 years or so, together with 60% of the fens, and 50% of the heathlands, and the percentage lost is as high in other natural habitats. In France alone, it is estimated that an incredible 10,000 hectares of wetland habitat are destroyed every year.

Conservation on a broad scale depends upon political decisions, huge financial deals, and

A bee orchid growing on a roadside verge.

A wetland nature reserve with a permanent hide from which to watch birds.

multi-national conglomerates. But there *are* things we can do as individuals.

• make sure that you do not injure or kill any animals, or uproot any plants while looking at wildlife, and don't disturb anything unnecessarily. Follow the country code.

• make your garden a haven for wildlife by banning sprays and putting out food in winter. Encourage plants which attract birds and insects and put up nestboxes.

• join your local organization for conserving nature. The more support they have, both financially and in numbers of members, the more they can show the decision-makers and politicians what needs doing.

• take part in voluntary work at weekends or in holidays on nature reserves or in national parks, to help with the vital tasks of management. Such jobs never seem like work when you are doing them with a crowd. Tire yourself out and get dirty – you'll enjoy it!

• tell people about the value of wildlife and the interesting things to be found locally.

• never give up. There is always something that can be done, especially if you work with other people who are interested.

KEEPING NOTES

An important part of being a good naturalist is keeping detailed records and notes. You should always have a small notebook with you, preferably hard-backed to make it easier to write in, together with a pencil. Pencils are better than pens since they still write when it is wet, and they work at any angle, when pens often give up on you. It is useful to have a supply of polythene bags, too – one to put your notebook plus your hand and a pencil in, so you can write when it is raining; and the remainder for collecting anything of interest.

You can use notes to help you identify things later – after all, you cannot carry field guides to everything with you! For example, you can make notes on the shape, colour and habits of a large moth you come across, or the detailed plumage of an unfamiliar bird. You can also use the notebook to make records of what you find, from lists of birds seen or flowers recorded, to descriptions such as 'a pile of old chemical canisters seen in ditch by the old windmill' for later reference. Include sketches or maps to illustrate what you are writing about, and later you can either use the information yourself, or take it to someone else if you need help.

You will probably use quite a few notebooks. Remember to put the starting and finishing date on the cover of each and to number them consecutively. In this way, it is much easier to find any information that you need, and they build up into a useful reference library.

A hedgehog, a frequent garden visitor, in search of slugs in a garden at night in spring.

A close-up photograph of marsh helleborine orchid shows how beautiful its flowers are.

Nature photography

Most people have, thankfully, given up shooting, collecting, or killing animals. Instead they have turned to photographing and observing them. It is not an easy option, however, and getting really good nature pictures is very challenging.

A good camera is essential. Try buying an older second-hand model to minimize the cost. The best sort is a single-lens reflex (SLR), where you view through the same lens that you photograph through; all SLRs have lenses that can be changed; a telephoto can be fitted for more distant wildlife, or special lenses for close-up work. Start with the basic camera, and build up a collection of lenses that you need for the subjects that interest you most.

The range of techniques to learn is endless, and there is always room for improvements, so buy a good book on the subject. Here are a few points to remember:

- hold your camera as steadily as possible, and support it on something if you can;
- try visiting your local nature reserve to see what is there, and if there is a permanent hide for bird-watching, use it;
- be patient and careful, and don't take masses of pictures before you are ready;
- always learn from your mistakes, and try to decide where you went wrong, and what to do about it.

Linear nature reserves

The countryside of western Europe has changed greatly in the last 30 years or so, becoming steadily less hospitable for wildlife. One way in which man has helped to conserve nature is by creating 'linear' features, such as canals, motorways, and railway lines. These act as havens for many forms of wildlife, and they are especially useful in two different ways.

First, they are like islands of wilder habitat in areas that may otherwise be built up, or very heavily farmed. For instance, canals can provide homes for masses of aquatic animals that might find nowhere else suitable for miles around, and motorway verges frequently have wildflowers, such as cowslips, that have gone from the barley fields around them.

But they help in another way, too. All these linear features act as corridors for the movement of wildlife – including plants – from one area to another. This may be a daily movement, as, for example, a badger moving into a town each night to find food, retreating to his rural lair at night; or it may be a slower movement, as new species colonize and spread along the lines. A butterfly, for example, unless it is one of the strong-flying migrants, will be reluctant to venture out into arable fields, or across built-up areas, but it will move for miles along hedges or paths. In this way, it can find and colonize new areas.

Keep an eye on these linear features, even though they are often man-made. They are very important, and we need to conserve as many as possible.

Right: *Oxford ragwort has spread into urban habitats in many areas, from its original home in Sicily.*

Right: *Kestrels are a familiar feature of motorway verges nowadays, where they hunt for small mammals.*

Below: *The newly seeded verge of a motorway is a mass of flowers for the first few years.*